A JERK ON ONE END

Robert Hughes

A JERK ON ONE END

Reflections of a Mediocre Fisherman

With Illustrations by
Andrew McLean

THE HARVILL PRESS
LONDON

First published in the USA in 1999 by The Ballantine Publishing Group,
a division of Random House, Inc.

First published in Great Britain in 1999 by
The Harvill Press
2 Aztec Row, Berners Road
London N1 0PW

www.harvill.com

1 3 5 7 9 8 6 4 2

A CIP catalogue record is available from the British Library

ISBN 1 86046 703 2

Designed and typeset in Caslon
at Libanus Press, Marlborough, Wiltshire

Printed and bound in Great Britain by Butler & Tanner Ltd
at Selwood Printing, Burgess Hill

To Doris

There was a young lady of Wales,
Who caught a large fish without scales;
When she lifted the hook
She exclaimed: "Only look!"
That extatic young lady of Wales.

— EDWARD LEAR, IN
A BOOK OF NONSENSE (1846)

ACKNOWLEDGMENTS

OVER THE YEARS I HAVE FISHED WITH MANY PEOPLE and learned something from them all. But I particularly want to set down my debt and gratitude to four of them. In alphabetical order, then. To John Alexander, the Texas Terror. To Peter Duchin, companion and best of friends on many a fly-fishing excursion to Alaska and to northern Quebec. To Henry Kravis, who for the past few years in Colorado has shown me a level of trout fishing (and of hospitality) whose existence I had scarcely even imagined. And to Alan Shields, skipper of *Stinkpot IV*, for getting me back into sea fishing after I moved to Long Island.

The quotations from Po Chu-I's *Fishing in the Wei River*, John Donne's *Sermon on Matthew 4:18–20*, and James Saunders's *The Compleat Fisherman* are taken from that excellent compendium *The Magic Wheel: An Anthology of Fishing in Literature*, edited by David Profumo and Graham Smith (1985).

I

SALT WATER

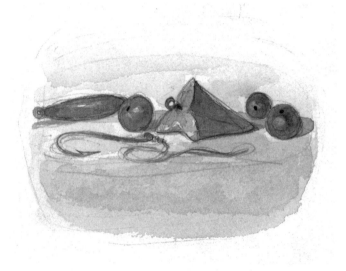

"A JERK ON ONE END OF A LINE, WAITING FOR a jerk on the other." Such is one of the classic folk definitions of fishing. It echoes Samuel Johnson's description of the sport as a stick and a string, with a worm on one end and a fool on the other. And who can doubt its truth? In some ways it's a ridiculous human passion. I keep a fishing boat on Shelter Island at the far end of Long Island in New York State, where I live. It is an open, centre-console eight-metre Mako, built in 1979. It cost $12,000 when I bought it, secondhand, in 1981. Every year it costs me about $4,000 in dockage charges (six months of the year) and haulage and storage (the other six). I am not mechanically minded, and what lies under the cowling of its now aging 1988 Evinrude 225 is as complete a mystery to me as the meaning of the inscriptions on a Mayan stela. If it broke down at sea, I would be utterly at a loss. Its maintenance I leave to the experts at the boatyard, who charge about

$50 an hour for the work. It guzzles petrol at an alarming rate, and has a complicated oil-mixture system with an alarm beeper hooked into it. Of late, this beeper has taken to going off – a shrill, moronic warble that stops as mysteriously as it starts – when the engine seems to be running perfectly, nothing discernible is wrong, and the oil tank is more than half full. It usually happens on a hard-running tide in the strait between Orient Point and Plum Island or, even worse, in the big rip known as The Race off Fishers Island, 30 kilometres from home, thus filling me with a sense of incompetence and dread at the prospect of drifting helplessly off into the deep Atlantic. This diminishes the feeling of oceanic peace and oneness with the cosmos that the more mystical-minded fishing writers claim to be the reward of their sport. All in all, were I to balance the market value of the fish I catch in a year against the expense of catching them, I would say I was spending about $120 per kilogram on bluefish, which, scaled and filleted, can be had in the local store for about $8.99.

And this is to ignore what other kinds of fishing cost. The last time I passed a weekend pursuing tarpon in the Florida Keys, for instance, there were the air tickets to Miami and back, the car rental, the motel in Islamorada with its corroded faucets and the sexual galumphing coming from the other side of the thin wall, the boat charter and guiding costs: all, in the end, for one brief connection with one large silver fish, which made two reel-burning runs, treated me to a frenzied display of clattering, shining leaps, spat out the fly, and vanished.

And yet it would be contemptible to complain. Fishing largely consists of not catching fish; failure is as much a part of the sport as knee injuries are of football.

I have fished a good deal of my life. Not professionally, of course, and not with enough dedication to qualify as "expert", however you might define that. But constantly enough, and with sufficient enthusiasm, to call myself an addict. I grew up on Sydney Harbour, in Australia. In the late 1940s and early 1950s its waters had plenty of fish in them. (Today they do again; it was during the 1960s and 1970s that the harbour waters became so polluted that most of the fish vanished, their spawn poisoned by industrial effluents. They have since made a comeback.) Mostly I would fish with a hand line from a pier that stuck out into Rose Bay at the bottom of Cranbrook Road, where our house was. Always, one could see small fish – mainly yellowtail, a species of jack – swimming in the clear green water around the pier's worn and splintery pilings. One would take a pellet of stale bread, wet it with spit, and mould it around a tiny hook tied to a fine monofilament line with no sinker. The white scrap would sink slowly, slowly in the water. The trick was to take up as much slack as possible without lifting the bait up. With luck, one of the little fish would charge it and there would be the electric jolt of contact with a creature utterly unlike oneself, which would then be pulled in, its silver body frantically quivering. On the bottom, with a sinker, one could also catch leatherjackets – a small and rather torpid triggerfish, named for the toughness of its hide – and the occasional red bream, the baby version of the giant red snapper that inhabited deeper waters, off the harbour's headlands. Since my mother generally refused to cook these small victims, they were given to the cat or ended up in the garbage. Only once did I catch anything resembling a game fish, when by the sheerest fluke a small passing bonito grabbed my bait just as it hit the water. It couldn't have weighed more than two or three kilograms, but I still have the faint white scars on my index finger left by the hand line. 50 years later they have faded to near invisibility, but I can still see them. I couldn't have been more pleased if they had been duelling scars. Sucking my cuts, admiring the dying fish as its colours faded on the dock, surrounded by a ring of awed kids my own age, I felt the first surge of triumph in my life.

I had never felt this sense of prowess from any other sport. I was neither good nor bad at athletics, just skinny, unmotivated and fast in spurts, and I rather disliked team games, especially rugby, at which I was hopelessly bad. My idea of a contact sport was chess. Among the kids at school I had the largely deserved reputation of being an intellectual snob and a smart-arse. Guilty as charged. Fishing enabled me to be alone; to dream, yet with the senses on full alert. It saved me, to some degree, from the guilt of not fitting in with the peculiarly intense collectivity of boarding school. Nobody was watching.

Other sports made my failures conspicuous: the cricket ball scooped into the air, an easy catch for the hostile

fielder; my humiliating fumble of the baton in a relay race. But you did not fail at fishing, even if you caught nothing; you just "had a bad day" because the fish didn't cooperate. Years later, in the late 1960s, while reading Leonardo da Vinci's Notebooks in order to prepare for a book that I wound up never writing, I came across this sentence: *Se sei solo sarai tutto tuo* – "If you are alone, you are entirely your own man." Fishing is, or should be, a thoughtful business. I was often told that rugby players think, but on the field I couldn't – I was too consumed with terror that if the greasy rugby ball ever reached me on the wing, the phalanx of giant country boys from western New South Wales would bear down on me with their knobbly knees, aiming to mash me into the mud.

I cannot think of a single benefit I received from having to play rugby, beyond a thin veneer of stoicism produced not by genuine courage but by the fear of being thought a wimp. But there were several ways in which fishing formed my imagination as a child. It taught me something of the craft of handling time; it helped me overcome the inbuilt impatience of childhood, and I was an impatient kid who wanted quick results, a fast track from desire to its satisfaction.

You cannot hurry fishing, because it is the fish, not you, that decides the tempo. This continuous absorptive contact with the harbour turned me towards the literature of the sea. Most Australian schoolkids of my generation were taught to memorise a poem of John Masefield's that began, "I must go down to the seas again, to the lonely

sea and the sky". But on digging a collected Masefield out
of my father's library, I was enthralled by "Dauber", his
long narrative poem – largely autobiographical, though
I didn't realise that at the time – about a boy who wants
to be a painter but runs away to sea on a four-master
bound for Cape Horn across the Atlantic, where he
meets his death. I read *Lord Jim*, and Joshua Slocum's
memoirs of his solitary voyage around the world in the
little sloop *Spray*; and, best of all for its direct appeal to
a thirteen-year-old boy, Rudyard Kipling's wonderful
Bildungsroman of another thirteen-year-old's passage to
early manhood through the rough comradeship of a
Grand Banks schooner's crew, *Captains Courageous*. There
were even poems about Sydney Harbour itself, which
strongly affected me: Kenneth Slessor's "Five Bells", his
great elegy for a bohemian friend who drowned after
falling overboard from a Manly ferry with his pockets
full of beer bottles – the Australian *Lycidas*, as someone
called it; and, hardly less suggestive, his evocation of a
retired Pacific mariner, "Captain Dobbin", living out his
last years in a brick villa by the harbour and logging the
comings and goings of its sea traffic:

> For at night, when the stars mock themselves with
>   lanterns,
> So late the chimes blow loud and faint
> Like a hand shutting and unshutting over the bells,
> Captain Dobbin, having observed from bed
> The lights, like a great fiery snake, of the *Comorin*

Going to sea, will note the hour
For subsequent recording in his gazette.

But the sea is really closer to him than this,
Closer to him than a dead, lovely woman,
For he keeps bits of it, like old letters,
Salt tied up in bundles,
Or pressed flat,
What you might call a lock of the sea's hair,
So Captain Dobbin keeps his dwarfed memento,
His urn-burial, a chest of mummied waves,
Gales fixed in print, and the sweet dangerous countries
Of shark and casuarina-tree,
Stolen and put in coloured maps,
Like a flask of sea-water, or a bottled ship,
A schooner caught in a glass bottle;
But Captain Dobbin keeps them in books . . .
So nightly he sails from shelf to shelf,
Or to the quadrants, dangling with rusty screws,
Or the hanging-gardens of old charts,
So old they bear the authentic protractor-lines,
Traced in faint ink, as fine as Chinese hairs.

Over the flat and painted atlas-leaves
His reading-glass would tremble,
Over the fathoms, pricked in tiny rows,
Water shelving to the coast.
Quietly the bone-rimmed lens would float
Till, through the glass, he felt the barbed rush

Of bubbles foaming, spied the albacores,
The blue-finned admirals . . .

I longed to see those albacores, those blue-finned
admirals. And I can never see an old brassbound quadrant
in a junk store without thinking of Captain Dobbin and
his author. Under such influences, the Pacific opened to
my boy's imagination as a sort of epic space, charted by
others but not experienced by me, and I yearned to know
it. This longing has never been satisfied, and now that I
am 60, I do not expect it to be. My family had no boat, no
maritime background. My father had been a flier – one of
the pioneers who flew their Sopwith Camels and Bristol
Fighters against the Germans in World War I – but he
couldn't have been less interested in boating, or in any
kind of saltwater fishing. So I rarely got out of the harbour
and was confined to its foreshores, rocks and piers. No
matter; though I didn't really know it at the time, I was
getting an education in seeing and discriminating. To
fish at all, even at a humble level, you must notice things:
the movement of the water and its patterns, the rocks, the
seaweed, the quiver of tiny scattering fish that betrays a
bigger predator under them. Time on the pier taught me
to concentrate on the visual, for fishing is intensely visual
even – perhaps especially – when nothing is happening.
It is easy to look, but learning to *see* is a more gradual
business, and it sneaks up on you unconsciously, by stealth.
The sign that it is happening is the fact that you are
not bored by the absence of the spectacular. And Sydney

Harbour had its own character. It was not an Arcadian bay, but a big, variegated industrial port, full of heavy-duty maritime structures as well as small sandy coves and virgin headlands of tumbled rocks. I came to love the straightforward, functional shapes of old rust-streaked hulls and pylons, buoys and bollards, wooden posts and docks. These demotic forms intrigued me in a way that the genteel artefacts of upper-middle-class Australian life, the "good" furniture and the silverware produced on special occasions, did not; they had a strength that went beyond questions of taste, and ever since, I have delighted in vernacular, practical objects, things made straightforwardly for use in work. Nothing about them was superfluous. Each had a history of use, which I liked to ponder and even fantasise about: the decaying hull half sunk in the sand of Rose Bay beach, the mysterious, rusting, rivet-bound cylinder that might have been a buoy or a steam boiler. "Objects gross and the unseen soul are one," wrote Walt Whitman in "A Song for Occupations" (1881), his paean to American craft and making.

I also became aware of a kind of fishing that was entirely beyond me, and to which I hardly dared aspire. Big-game fishing in Australia was in its raw beginnings 50 years ago. It required boats and tackle that were so specialised, so difficult to come by and so costly as to be beyond the reach of most Australians. But the waters of Sydney – both inside the harbour and outside in the Pacific – held an abundance of sharks, and these possessed an iconic status in Australian imagination, because they were our

only big carnivores, the only creatures that posed a threat
to human life. The land had its dangerous reptiles and
insects, but nothing that walked, slithered or flew was
going to actually gobble you up, except for the saltwater
crocodile, *Crocodylus porosus*, whose habitat lay thousands of
kilometres away in the tropical north. In the sea, however,
it was different. There one might find the great white,
the mako, the tiger, the grey nurse, the hammerhead – or,
possibly, they might find you. Since the population of
Sydney was largely amphibious, and liked then as now to
go swimming during its lunch hour, the man-eater loomed
large in civic imagination – while in practice it ate few
men (or women or children), it was always *there*, a trigger
of latent fear. The beaches inside the harbour were ringed
with shark-proof nets or enclosed with iron mesh; on the
ocean beaches, vigilant lifeguards scanned the surf from
wooden towers, looking for the distant black chip of a
fin cutting the water. There were a few laconic heroes
who specialised in catching sharks with thick hand lines
from rowboats. One of them, in defiance of all caution, did
so from the rocks at Bondi Beach and killed scores of them
over the years. But only people who lived at Bondi were
likely to witness these struggles; I never did. The one place
where you could actually see the finny criminal close up
was the wharf station at Watsons Bay, just inside the arm
of South Head, where the Sydney big-game fishing club
strung up its catches to weigh them on a steelyard.

When a big shark was towed in behind a boat, it was
the nearest thing to a public hanging. The word would

begin to spread as soon as the fishermen docked. The nearby pub and the fish-and-chip shops would empty. Before the shark was even halfway out of the water a crowd would have assembled to see the malefactor receive its final humiliation. 200 or 300 watchers were common: pink sunburned fathers squinting in the afternoon light, mums in floral print dresses, kids spooning Peters ice-cream out of paper cups. A family spectacle, like Tyburn in the 1700s. Sometimes the shark would still be alive, and it was the vitality that fascinated me. Four kilograms of fish, four metres long, had been dragged thrashing to a standstill way out in the ocean. They had gaffed it and got a tailrope on it. Then, commonly, it had been shot several times in the head with a heavy rifle or a rusty shotgun loaded with ball, to quiet it down. Then they had towed it by the tail, the water sluicing backwards through its gill slots – enough to drown any fish, you'd think – with its blood running in a dilute stream in the wake, sharp dark crimson fading out to a faint pink, all those kilometres back to the dock.

As the tailrope was hooked to the lifting chain and the winch began to clatter, the oldies on the wharf would produce their laconic yarns of dread for the twelve-year-olds. *You should never haul a big shark into the boat if you have any choice about it. You think he's dead, but he's not. He's just playing possum. He'll bite your weewee off faster than you can say "Joe Stalin", sonny, and take your arse with it as well. Me mate Jack, he had his back broken by a mako when it woke up in the cockpit. Three months in Saint Vincent's. You can't fool with the bastards. Better stand back.*

And we did. As the shark rose out of the water I would be frozen by a delicious terror that, I would learn from Edmund Burke a decade later, is the root of the sublime. Ugly as sin, with its stomach protruding from its jaws, pressed out by vertical gravity; and yet as beautiful as Lucifer in its completeness – a mighty eating machine. Quite often it would give one contorted thrash and bite the wharf, sometimes leaving a tooth or two in the iron-hard timber: the criminal uttering a last curse from the scaffold. After hanging for a while, with its weight and the boat's name chalked on its now dry flank, it would be let down, dragged through the water to the beach in front of what is now Doyle's seafood restaurant, and cut up, just as Georgian murderers had been delivered to the anatomising surgeons. Its meat went for fertilizer, probably: nobody in Sydney wanted to eat an old shark, though smaller ones were sold in fish markets under the euphemistic name of "flake". Sometimes, even then, the shark didn't seem to know it was dead. I once saw the heart cut out of a big mako: a shiny pink lobe of muscle, 45 centimetres long. It continued to convulse and beat on the beach for twenty minutes after it was separated from the body, as though it were trying to get back down the sand into the water. So much for those comic strips in which Dick Daring finished off a shark underwater with a well-placed stab of his knife. You might as well take on a tank with a teaspoon.

Without reducing my enthusiasm for fishing, such gory sights had, I now realise, a permanent effect on me.

They increased the fascination the sea had for me – that mysterious, wild world below the surface, filled with only superficially familiar creatures whose existence was so utterly remote from that of human beings. The fundamental experience of fishing consists of dropping a line into the unknown. You can guess at what is down there; you can make your best estimates based on tide, habitat, feeding patterns and so forth; but you do not really know. Whatever takes your hook therefore has a character of revelation, even if it's only a flounder. It may be edible or not; thorny, spiny or beautifully sleek; equipped with gnashing jaws or relatively passive; but there is always, assuming that you aren't sight-fishing, the magic moment when the thing struggling on your line down there could be *anything*. The similarities between the writer's work and the angler's need not be laboured, but they exist. The writer lets down his or her hook into the deposit of memory and experience, the semiconscious fluid – not the dark, abyssal unconscious, which is out of reach, but the tidal zone where word, phrase, idea and memory circulate in a kind of half-light, forming their unpredicted patterns. With luck, you bring something up. If it is undersize, you toss it back.

In earlier times, the inscrutability of the sea bred fantasy. The water's surface was the limit of the rational world. Below it, before the age of hydrography, ichthyology and the aqualung, was the abode of demons, monsters, and every sort of blood-freezing deformity: a zone without limits in which imagination could run free.

The biblical archetype of these sea beasts was Leviathan.
By the sixteenth century they had bred and mutated
without limits, and were to the Mannerist imagination
what space aliens are to us. Here is Edmund Spenser, in
Canto XII of *The Faerie Queene*, listing the horrors his sea
voyagers confront after their passage between quicksand
and whirlpool.

> an hideous hoast arrayd
> Of huge Sea Monsters, such as living sense dismayd.
>
> Most ugly shapes, and horrible aspects,
> Such as Dame Nature selfe mote [might] feare to see,
> Or shame, that ever should so fowle defects
> From her most cunning hand escaped be;
> All dreadful pourtraicts of deformitee:
> Spring-headed *Hydraes*, and sea-shouldring Whales,
> Great whirlpools, which all fishes make to flee,
> Bright *Scolopendraes*, arm'd with silver scales,
> Mighty *Monoceros*, with immeasured tayles.
>
> The dreadfull Fish, that hath deserv'd the name
> Of Death, and like him lookes in dreadfull hew,
> The griesly Wasserman, that makes his game
> The flying ships with swiftnesse to pursew,
> The horrible Sea-Satyre, that doth shew
> His fearefull face in time of greatest storme,
> Huge *Ziffius*, whom Mariners eschew
> No less than rocks (as travellers informe)
> And greedy *Rosmarines* with visages deforme.

All these, and thousand thousands many more,
And more deformed Monsters thousand fold,
With dreadfull noise, and hollow rombling rore,
Came rushing in the fomy waves enrold,
Which seem'd to fly for fear, them to behold:
No wonder, if these did the knight appall;
For all that here on earth we dreadful hold,
Be but as bugs to fearen babes withall,
Compared to creatures in the seas entrall [entrails,
    inner parts].

Hydras were giant squid; "huge *Ziffius*" was the swordfish, *Xiphias gladius* (the Greek and Latin words for
"sword" conjoined), which had a reputation for driving its
bill into the hulls of boats; but who knows what a grisly
Wasserman or a greedy Rosmarine might have been?
(Methinks I see them on a Manhattan office directory:
Rosmarine and Wasserman, divorce attorneys.) Sea creatures mutated into wonders in the minds of those who
had never seen one. The classic example is the mermaid,
who is often said (by those seeking rational explanations
of irrational fears and desires) to have originated with the
manatee or dugong, though a sailor would need to be
either very shortsighted or quite deranged with randiness
to mistake one of these fat mammals for a tempting water
nymph. People had been seeing and catching dolphins all
over the waters of the world by the eighteenth century,
and yet the standard dolphin of the visual arts bore no
relation to the real, sleek, graceful creature that followed

ships, which artists, as Benjamin Franklin complained in
his shipboard diary of an Atlantic passage in 1726, had
"improved into a crooked monster with a head and eyes
like a bull, a hog's snout, and a tail like a blown tulip".

Today these mythological forms of marine otherness
are fading from the culture – though they have not
entirely gone. They reappear in the images of creatures
that practically none of us are going to see except in
photographs – the phosphorescent, hair-tailed weirdnesses
of the abyssal depths, the barely studied fauna that cluster
around boiling volcanic clefts on the ocean floor, the living
fossil of a coelacanth dragged by the merest fluke from
deep water and paraded on a wheelbarrow through an
Indonesian port market. Thanks to them, the sea remains
in some ways richer in anomalies than the Middle Ages or
the Renaissance ever imagined. It is a somewhat abstract,
conceptual strangeness, since the ordinary fisherman has
no contact with such beings.

In America a century ago, it was otherwise. Not only
were American fisheries amazingly abundant, but they
held forms of marine life that no sport fisherman had
ever dared attack before. The possibility of heroic, almost
mythic, encounter was still there, latent in American
nature. Henry Longfellow presumably sensed this when
he had his Indian hero Hiawatha go after the sturgeon
Nahma, "king of fishes", all alone in a birch canoe with a
line of twisted cedar bark; Nahma, as though in a rehearsal
for *Jaws*, is provoked into leaping upwards from the depths
and swallowing both Hiawatha and his canoe. (As a matter

of record, sturgeon can't swallow people, let alone boats, not that it mattered to Longfellow.) From the 1890s on, a new and particularly American genre of fishing writing came into its own: fishing as dangerous safari, in pursuit of enormous prey. The surface of the sea – Nova Scotia in the north, but especially the waters of Florida and the islands and reefs of the Caribbean – became a watery veldt traversed by wild giants such as the various billfish (black marlin, blue marlin, striped marlin, broadbill swordfish), the shark (not something you deliberately fished for at first, but were bound to contend with), the giant bluefin tuna, and the tarpon. In part, the pursuit of these creatures was made possible by technical advances in tackle – stronger rods, more capacious reels, tougher line. But it also came out of a peculiar kind of will that had nothing to do with the older, more contemplative ideals of angling. There is a manic quality to some of the late-nineteenth-century writing about saltwater fishing, produced by "great white hunters" such as Charles Frederick Holder (1851–1915): anything that swims, no matter how harmless or inedible, becomes an object of obsessive pursuit merely because it is big and unfamiliar. If you read Holder in *Big Game at Sea* (1908) on hunting a manta ray to death, for instance – hurling lance after lance into the enormous beast until, weakened and disorientated, it bleeds to death in the shallows off the Florida coast – you are struck by two main features of his narrative: first, the undeniable pluck and tenacity it must have taken to attempt such a hunt, but second, the utter pointlessness of the whole exercise.

The early high-water mark of American big-game fishing came in the 1930s, when a small group of mainly American enthusiasts – the equivalents of the African hunting guides of the late nineteenth century – shaped the sport to the point where, in 1940, Michael Lerner founded the International Game Fish Association (IGFA), which made the rules for heavy saltwater angling and still verifies and maintains its records. Some of them are remembered as the hook-and-line equivalents of Babe Ruth or Ben Hogan or Joe Louis: S. Kip Farrington, Zane Grey, Alfred Glassell (the first man to take a billfish that weighed more than a thousand pounds on rod and reel), and of course Ernest Hemingway.

The tackle they used was enormous. The London firm, Hardy, then the reigning rod maker, made a steel-core pole known as a "Zane Grey" that weighed nearly a kilogram and a half and was the first to sport roller guides, locking ferrules, and other amenities of today's rods. The ponderous Vom Hofe reels, wound with a kilometre of Ashaway line braided from Irish linen that terminated in a steel leader made by the same Roebling works that spun the cables for the Brooklyn Bridge, were like marine winches compared with modern gear. In fact, the rapid development of tackle worried Hemingway, who wrote in the introduction to Farrington's 1939 book on big-game fishing that the sport was in danger of being ruined by it, because it reduced the struggle involved in "a contest of strength and endurance between a man or a woman and an oversized fish".

The sporting essence of that struggle, as Hemingway set it forth, was the one whose elements are enshrined in the IGFA rules. The angler must bear the whole weight and pull of the fish by himself, holding the rod and reel in his own hands, with extra support from a harness across his back to which the gear could be attached. But he must not tie, rest or prop the rod against any part of the boat, because then "he is not fishing – the boat is fishing for him"; instead of fighting the angler, the tuna or marlin is towing the boat. Nobody else on board may touch the rod or reel until the fish is at the boat and it's time to grab the leader. Some kinds of tackle were expressly forbidden, such as the low-gear, two-handled reels, like the "coffee grinders" used for tightening sail sheets on racing yachts. These reels enabled the fisherman to literally crank in a big fish instead of "pumping" it – raising the rod and then winning a metre or two of line by winding while lowering it, a tiring technique that pits the angler's muscular strength against the weight and resistance of the prey.

No one who has not tried it should underestimate either the subtlety or the hardship of big-game fishing. To be tied into a large marlin that will rip hundreds of metres of line from the reel in an unstoppable plunge to the depths of the ocean, and then have to pump him up, metre by hard-won metre to the surface, only to have him sound again and force you to repeat the struggle while the boat is rolling in a strong cross-sea and your legs shake from hours of bracing them against the footrest of the fighting chair and your back muscles hurt and your left hand is numb from holding the rod grip and your right is an aching claw from turning the reel handle – this is one of the toughest forms of sport ever devised, and not to be scoffed at by those who have not done it.

It was far more extreme in the 1930s, when doughty American big-gamers such as Kip Farrington and Michael Lerner would go after Atlantic swordfish and giant bluefin tuna – in those days, any bluefin under 250 kilograms was jocosely classed as a "midget" – among the rocks and reefs of Nova Scotia, not in twelve-metre big-game boats but in small dories, each rowed by one man, equipped with homemade swivel fighting-chairs. With little or no inertia from the dories, which were light shells, it was the purest form of man-versus-fish angling, almost equally punishing to both.

This kind of fishing is no longer done, partly because it was so rough on the fisherman, but mainly because the fish are no longer there, whereas 60 years ago they schooled in incredible abundance. Farrington, in *Atlantic Game Fishing* (1939), casually mentions how Maine harpooners would go after giant bluefin tuna off Portland in that State in the 1930s. The hunter "hopes that if he misses the mark the dart will strike the fish beneath the one at which he aimed. These great fish are usually found in layers three or four feet deep, travelling like a flotilla of submarines. Over five hundred fish a year are brought into the Portland piers . . ." Nothing like this can be experienced in American waters today, or ever will be again.

Most fish become familiar if you go after them regularly.

Yet not completely so, for each fish is new, and there are moments when the sense of strangeness revives and sits bolt upright; these are among the high points of any fisher's career. The one I remember most vividly happened off Montauk, at the eastern tip of Long Island, in the summer of 1985. I was on an overnight trip to fish for tuna on the Canyon, a part of the continental shelf about 110 kilometres out in the Atlantic, in a no-frills offshore boat skippered by an artist friend, Alan Shields. After the long night's run out, the sun rose golden and glorious out of the Atlantic and the sea was flat calm; you could see the smallest ripple a kilometre away. We set the trolling lines and the "bird", a teaser with two wings that fluttered on the surface about 20 metres back from the stern and was supposed to excite the curiosity of the fish. That done, there was nothing to do but wait. An hour later, nothing had come up. And then Alan saw something dead ahead: the unmistakable sickle fins of two giant bluefin tuna, hovering on the light-stricken surface as though sunning themselves. They were perhaps a kilometre ahead. If we went past them at trolling speed, we would scare them down. There was probably no way of getting them to strike at a lure. But Alan wanted one of those fish (at the prices the Japanese were paying dockside at Montauk for prime bluefin, he could have paid for a whole season's fuel with it), and he decided to go after them with a harpoon. He would steer the boat and I would be up in the bow with the spear, whose detachable bronze head was already rigged to 100 metres of line and an orange balloon buoy. There

I would stand, intrepidly balanced out on the bow pulpit, as we treacherously sneaked up on the fish, and when I was within range, I would fling the harpoon into the tuna's vitals. There was only one snag about this arrangement. I am not Queequeg. My only experience of spearing sea creatures was sniggling eels with a small trident. Of hitting a tuna from above with a three-metre spear, I had no conception, and the fact that fishermen used to do this as a matter of course in their pursuit of tuna, swordfish and other monsters of the deep off Montauk meant very little to me. I was a rank novice, a mere art critic and (worse) an art critic who had read several cautionary yarns of what happens to incautious harpooners who happen by accident to get a coil of line around their arm, leg or even neck as it comes burning out of the tub, pulled by a quarter-tonne of potential sashimi, maddened with shock and pain, accelerating down and away into the oceanic abyss. Tuna can do 100 kilometres an hour. These thoughts hung before me as I drew closer to the fish, nervously balancing the shaft in my hand. I focused on the nearer fish. It seemed to hover in the water: the silver flanks, the dark blue back, not the leaden darkness of a dead fish, but alive, inexpressibly vital, the small dorsal finlets glowing yellow. Closer and closer. And then I caught its eye, that huge eye with its hypnotic black centre, evolved to capture every last photon in the deep sea. God, it occurred to me, was looking at me through that fish. I was frozen. Dimly I heard a voice from the flying bridge behind me: "Stick him! Stick him!" But I couldn't; I couldn't imagine throwing the harpoon. The eye had paralysed me. Later I would learn from other fishermen, such as Peter Matthiessen, that this was not an uncommon occurrence. *Never look at the tuna's eye*, ran the conventional wisdom. Or at a swordfish's, either, which is even larger and more hypnotic. But I will never forget the sight of that bluefin, in the splendour of its unreflective life, or how it slid out of sight with the merest quiver of its body, cleanly accelerating through the blue, gone forever. It took Alan some time to forgive me.

By then I had been fishing around Long Island for several years. My interest in angling had gone flat and dormant when I left Australia for Europe in the early 1960s. In Italy, where I lived for a while in the fishing village of Porto Ercole, there were few fish to catch; even 30-odd years ago, the waters of the Tyrrhenian Sea were so depleted by pollution and relentless dragnetting that a one-kilogram *dentice* or *spigola* would become the talk of the Bar Centrale. In England, where I settled later, I seldom moved outside London. No fishing there. But after I crossed to New York in 1970, fishing presented itself once again.

The eastern end of Long Island, three hours or less from Manhattan, was one of the world's great fisheries and, though considerably depleted, it still is. The angler's year there begins in April, when the "cocktail blues" – small bluefish – begin to show up in the bays and the flounder stir from their hibernation on the seabed, and it goes right through to the middle of November, when it gets too cold for me or any but the hardiest to fish from the beaches or from an open boat. Spotted silver weakfish (so called not for any debility, but because of the ease with which the hook tears from their mouth membranes) turn up in the early spring, and then there are runs of mackerel. In April the Greenport dock is crowded with Greek-Americans who come there to catch squid at night, with electric floodlights and jigs. In May and June the striped bass begin to appear. Bluefish last all summer and into the autumn, and by July the fluke (a flatfish, like a flounder only fiercer and more carnivorous, running up to five or six kilograms, at which size they justify their nickname of "doormats") are to be caught all over the Peconic Bay system. With the warming of the offshore water come the tuna, though in badly diminished numbers these days: yellowfin, albacore, the "false albacore" or bonito (known as "watermelons" for their thick, compact bodies and striped flanks), and the lord of them all, *Thunnus thynnus*, the Atlantic bluefin. The inshore fishing reaches a crescendo in September and October, with the schools of striped bass and still more bluefish, and the appearance of albacore and bonito in the bays.

The handsomest of all these fish, and the one most ardently pursued by anglers, is *Morone saxatilis*, the striped bass, with its silver-flanked body tinged with topaz bronze and striated by horizontal black lines, its fine proportions spoiled only, in the larger specimens, by a glutton's potbelly. It is also by far the best-tasting and the most amenable to any kind of cooking: poached, baked, grilled, fried or sliced into sashimi when absolutely fresh right out of the water. "An excellent fish," wrote Captain John Smith in 1614. "They are so large, the head of one will give a good eater a dinner, and for daintiness of diet they excell the Marybones [marrow bones] of Beefe ... I myselfe at the turning of the tyde have seen such multitudes passe ... that it seemed to me that one mighte go over their backs drishod." The best eating size – the "money fish", as professional seiners used to call them – is three or four kilograms, but they grow much bigger, to 30 or more. The heaviest recorded specimen was a 57-kilogram fish taken in 1891 in North Carolina. They were so common, and their migratory runs from their spawning grounds in the Chesapeake Bay system north along the Atlantic coast so huge, that for a time the English settlers of New England, taking their cue from the Indians, buried them in their fields as fertilizer. But as early as 1639 this practice was banned by the General Court of the Massachusetts Bay Colony – the first species-protection law ever passed in America. Striped bass also played a role in early American education, as in 1670 the Plymouth Colony used revenues from bass and mackerel to set up the New World's first public school.

One of the striper's great merits, from the angler's point of view, is its accessibility. In the southern Atlantic States they are known as "rockfish", because they prefer coastal waters and, with their muscular bodies and broad propeller tails, are superbly adapted to cope with the violent stresses of life among the reefs, rips and beach surf. Stripers are anadromous, "up-going", which means that they ascend rivers to spawn – 160 kilometres above the tidewater in the case of the Roanoke River's spawning grounds – and can live quite happily in fresh water. Each year they do a mass migration along the land's edge, from the Chesapeake up to New Jersey, New York, Massachusetts, and Maine, and then return to their wintering grounds in the south.

Sticking to the coast, they are easy to get at. At every point along their immemorial route, on every rock and headland and beach and in thousands of inshore boats, fishers are waiting for them, jigging, spinning, bait casting, trolling, sinker bouncing, and casting long streamer flies. This is quite a gauntlet to run, but since the bass do not venture far offshore they are not exposed to heavily industrial forms of fishing, the long lines and deep-sea nets that are decimating other species such as tuna. The greater danger to coastwise fish is chemical pollution from runoff and sea dumping – not only on the open shore but, especially, in their southern spawning grounds and nursery waters. *Morone saxatilis'* Atlantic range runs along the most heavily industrialised and intensively farmed coast in America, and the witch's cocktail of pesticides, fertilizers, heavy metals and ghastly polysyllabic chemical effluents that is sluiced and dumped from it almost beggars rational imagination. DDT, dieldrin, dibromo-chloropropane, PCBs, cadmium, arsenic, lead, hexachloro-benzene, cis-chlordane, mercury. All these and many more went into the seawater and from there into the livers, testes and ova of the bass. It is not surprising that

when John Coles wrote his admirable book *Striper* (1978) about the relations between *Morone saxatilis* and *Homo sapiens*, he felt driven to the most pessimistic of conclusions: "Ten years from now, at its current rate of decline, the striped bass . . . will have vanished as a viable species." But fortunately this didn't happen.

In the last decade, strict limits have been placed on the taking of striped bass on Long Island. The minimum keepable size was fixed at a little under a metre: an eight-kilogram fish, six years old (well into middle age, though tagged specimens have lived into their mid-20s), and tasting – so anglers grumbled – like a copy of the Sunday edition of the *New York Times*, rolled up and boiled. The size restrictions caused prolonged and bitter controversy. They were denounced as a mere cosmetic by those (including Peter Matthiessen, nature writer, novelist and a fisherman of long experience) who believed that the decline of the striper was due not to overfishing but to the chemical poisoning of the spawning grounds. Matthiessen wrote a powerful and evocative book, *Men's Lives* (1986), to defend the dwindling community of Long Island dory-seiners against charges brought by the sport-fishing lobby that it was they, not the amateur hook-and-liners, who put too much pressure on the bass population, and that in any case pollution was the real threat to the fish. Nobody could deny that pollution does their spawning and growth immense harm, but the fact is that the hardy and resilient bass have made a comeback in the last decade. Either their population crash was increased by a cyclical recession of unknown origin (this has been known to happen to bluefish as well as stripers) or else the massive catch of smaller specimens, mainly by hook-and-liners, really did tip the scales towards disaster. Whatever the case, since the size limits were imposed the bass population of eastern Long Island has recovered, and they are everywhere. This is one of the few really promising feats of wild-fish management that America has to show. Alas, the species that got driven out of business was the tiny band of dory-seiners who, like their ancestors for two centuries, had netted the Long Island beaches but, unlike the droves of sport-fishermen, were in no way responsible for the crash.

The staple of Long Island sport-fishing is *Pomatomus saltatrix*, the bluefish, the only representative of its family, the *Pomatomidae*. It assumes various names, depending on its age. Little ones are "snapper blues", young ones – up to a kilogram or so – are "cocktail blues" or "tailors", and then you have regular "blues". The really big ones – which go to six or seven kilograms – are "gorillas". It is exactly the same fish that is known as a *pesce turco* in Italy and a *lufer* in Turkey, as a "tailor" in Australia and an *anchova* in Brazil. It is the fish that everyone knows how to catch because, given its habits and temperament, you don't need to know anything to catch one. Charter captains with their freight of inexperienced weekend tourists go out in flotillas off Montauk and around Shagwong Reef, into The Race between Fishers Island and Great Gull lighthouse, and in Plum Gut between Orient Point and Plum Island. They run out their wire lines, each with a four-armed umbrella rig trailing hooks adorned with red and green surgical tubing and in come the blues. Wire-line trolling isn't fishing, it's winching. It doesn't deserve to be called a sport.

Jigging for blues is somewhat higher on the evolutionary scale. To do this, you snap a jig – a shiny, spindle-shaped metal lure weighing up to 225 grams – on to your wire leader, which is in turn tied to a fifteen-kilogram monofilament line. You then click the reel into free-spool, drop the jig over the side, and let it run down to the bottom, keeping your thumb on the spool to control backlash – a condition in which the spool turns faster than the line is going out, creating a horrible "bird's nest". You feel the bump as the jig hits the bottom. You see the line go slack for an instant. You throw the reel into gear and crank as fast as you can. What you are hoping for is not a delicate touch, but a violent thump, as though an animated concrete block had attached itself to your line. This is a bluefish, and you must now reel him in through 30 or so vertical metres of water, while the tidal rip carries your boat along. Once the blue is on the surface, you swing him inboard and drop him on the deck, where he must be approached with care and resolution. Reputedly, unlike most fish, this one can see out of water, and what he sees and will bite is the hand that caught him. You must grab the beast behind the gills, hold him hard, twist the hook out of his jaw (no delicate dentistry here), and skid him into the fish-well, then sluice down the blood, because it will dry as hard as crimson acrylic. Then run up against the tide, start your

drift, and jig again. It is not the most refined form of
fishing, but there is something agreeably basic and brutish
about it, and women, I have noticed, love it: it speaks to
the latent maenad in them.

The problem is not how to catch Long Island blues
but what to do with them afterwards. Catching one bluefish is like eating one french fry. If they are around, you
always end up with more than you need, and bluefish
are about as easy to give away in the summer as oversize
zucchini: it's a form of generosity that your friends despise.
They are an oily fish and don't freeze well – a late-season
gorilla blue, fattened and glutted by gorging on menhaden
and herring, is one of the greasiest brutes that swims.
The epicure would say that bluefish are not even much
good the day after they're caught, because their flesh is
attacked by its own enzymes and quickly turns mushy. It
is wholly pointless to buy them in a New York fish market,
because they have already been out of the water for days.
But caught in the morning, bled, gutted, filleted and laid
on the barbecue for lunch, with a handful of chives and
some lemon juice, they can be memorable.

The pleasures of eating them, though, pale beside
those of catching them. Blues are voracious beyond belief.
They're like Cuisinarts with fins, equipped with rows of
razor teeth. A school of blues tearing into a school of
baitfish on the surface is one of those spectacles that will
still all thoughts of the benevolence and peaceability of
Nature. It is manic, out-of-control *Mörderlust* – every fish
a Jack the Ripper. You can see a feeding school kilometres

away, from the birds – seagulls and terns wheeling and
hitting the water, scarfing up the mangled bits of smaller
fish that the blues are attacking. Oldtimers say that if
they're eating menhaden you can smell them, too – the oil
in the baitfish, released by the blues' jaws, makes a slick
on the water. I can't claim to have noticed this, but right
under the boat I have seen bluefish, glutted with their
prey, vomit it all up like Roman gluttons before gorging
again. When in such frenzies, blues will strike at practically
anything from a streamer fly to a Budweiser can, and if
they miss it, they will strike again. Once hooked, they fight
with a furious all-out abandon that makes the classier and
more fastidious striped bass look relatively sluggish. "If
the species grew to the size of a bluefin tuna," declares the
sober entry in *McClane's Fishing Encyclopedia*, "nothing
could stand before it in the oceans of the world." No,
indeed, it would be a sort of *T. rex* with fins, indomitably
savage. Luckily for swimmers, the bluefish does not get
that big – the largest recorded one, a 20-kilogram monster,
was caught in a net off the coast of Africa, and the hook-
and-line record, just under fifteen kilograms, was taken in
Hatteras Inlet, North Carolina, in 1972.

No prestige, therefore, attaches to catching a bluefish.
Often you have no say in the matter. It has happened, to
my annoyance, when casting a fly for false albacore. These
small members of the tuna family, the scombroids, turn up
in the Long Island bay system in late summer and autumn.
Getting near them is very much a matter of luck. They
travel in small schools and surface quite suddenly; then

they dive again and vanish, and there is no way of knowing when they'll re-emerge. So you have to be quick and accurate, and lay the fly in front of them as soon as you see them. Doing this while wobbling on the casting platform of a six-metre Keys flatboat in a moderate chop, with the wind over your wrong shoulder, is a test. At my level of skill, I can do it perhaps once in six tries – and you don't get six shots at albacore in an ordinary morning. Then, due to the unspeakable perversity of fate, the fish that grabs the fly turns out to be a solitary bluefish that gatecrashed the school of albies; by the time it is in the boat, juddering and glaring at you with its yellow assassin's eyes, the albacore are somewhere over the horizon. I have never yet caught a bonito, or so much as hooked an albacore, on a fly-rod. But next year will be different.

The excitement of connecting with a fish is in pro-portion to the hours of tedium that surround it, and the extreme case of this is another form of saltwater angling: fishing for tarpon. You can get blasé about blues, even about stripers, but tarpon – never. The tarpon, *Megalops atlanticus*, is a giant archaic herring, which grows to 100 kilograms or so. It is quite widely distributed on both sides of the Atlantic, from the Florida Keys down the Mexican coast, and on the other side along the flank of Africa. There, it attains great size but is rarely pursued by foreign anglers, who are understandably nervous of being shot in error by some AK47-wielding teenager in the latest civil war in Sierra Leone. African anglers, their economy being what it is, can rarely afford tarpon gear, so the fish is safe there. It is hardly less secure on the coast of the Americas, but for other reasons. The food value of a tarpon is nil; its skeleton is a web of sharp, interwoven bones, and the flesh between them, when cooked, tastes singularly uninteresting. Its sport value as a fly-fisher's target, though, is unbeatable. This statement is in code. "Sport value" means that the fish is not only inedible but insanely expensive to pursue, and, if hooked, practically impossible to get to the boat – unless it jumps into it of its own accord, breaking an angler's leg in the process, as it has been known to do. (A few anglers have actually been killed by falling tarpon.) Of course, tarpon can be taken by trolling, or with live bait – but then, I have seen Caribbean kids catching bonefish from a jetty in Grand Turk with hand lines and rusty hooks baited with conch. Such rudimentary means are spurned by fly-rodders, who want to make life as hard as it can possibly be made.

The first stop on the *via crucis* of humiliation, then, is one of those specialised stores that sell fly-fishing gear of such cost and technological refinement that it feels a bit like shopping for a Formula One car. Every tarpon wannabe has a favourite store; mine is the Urban Angler, in New York City. Procure a three-metre, twelve-weight, three-piece carbon-Kevlar-graphite-Kryptonite Sage or Loomis rod ($600 or so) and a suitable reel. "Suitable" means that it must have room for a great deal of backing and cost not less (and preferably much more) than another $600. A tarpon reel needs a drag system that won't fuse into a blob when the fish runs, and hence must be made

of semi-precious metals and recondite alloys used only in
the brakes of Ferraris or, perhaps, the entrails of the space
shuttle. Then backing, and fly-line, and leaders, and flies,
and a large tube of sunscreen, and a pair of those Polaroid
glasses that cost, inch for inch, the same as a mediaeval
stained-glass window in Sotheby's . . . well, it could have
been worse. You might have wanted to set yourself up for
tuna. You are getting off relatively cheap, though this, as
President Clinton might have said upon his sworn oath,
depends on what you mean by *relatively*.

Now you are in, let's say, Islamorada, Florida. You have
booked a guide and boat for three days. The first day was
overcast and rainy, with a sharp chop on the water, and
there was no point in even trying to go out, since the only
way to catch a tarpon on fly is to see it coming from afar
and to cast to it; no fish can be seen in this leaden murk.
You therefore spent the day reading an improving book,
snoozing in the motel room, and eating conch fritters in a
redneck bar, a routine punctuated by reassuring phone
calls from your guide, who knows that tomorrow will be
great. The second day was, if anything, worse and windier.
But that night the front passes through, and the dawn
of the third day looks like a picture postcard, gold, blue,
and calm. Filled with the unreasoning optimism that is
both the angler's folly and his main defence against going
wholly cuckoo, you meet Bud or Jake or Billy Bob down
at the marina. His craft is an open, low-slung, Keys
casting-boat, like a slipper six metres long, with a poling-
platform raised over its big outboard. Useless in the open

sea, it is beautifully adapted to the shallow maze of cuts and channels where tarpon cruise. It skims for miles over the flats, hardly raising a wake. Your fate is determined; it is all in the hands of the guide. Eventually he stops where, being an expert, he knows tarpon will be: at the edge of a channel where they will come through, singly or in pods of five or ten, looking for food. He drives a long fibreglass pole into the shallow bottom and ties the boat to it. Now you need only wait, as your excitement burns down into stoic resignation, while nothing happens and the skull-frying sun climbs higher into the sky. It is futile to repine.

Sometimes, however, they do appear. The guide can see them but you cannot, because you hardly know what you are looking for until it's too late. "Five or six at one o'clock, 100 feet out", he drawls, with the merest whisper of an exclamation mark. You must now try to spot them through the dazzle of light on the water, and eventually you do: slender, dark logs, much smaller than they ought to look, coming straight at you across the confusing moiré pattern of the flat bottom. Meanwhile you are frantically stripping line from the reel, getting ready to throw the fly. What you should do next, calmly, deftly and without delay, is put a 25-metre shot a couple of metres in front of the lead fish and then start stripping line in so that it sees the fly moving through the water, mistakes it for a small fish, and hits. Fat chance. Flooded with adrenalin and buck fever, you do everything wrong. The line has got under your sneaker because, stupidly, you moved your foot, and it falls short. Or the fly drops behind the fish. Or

the hook, thanks to your bad backcast, snags your shirt
or your earlobe. *Il mondo è pieno*, wrote Leonardo, *d'infinite
ragioni che non furono mai in isperienza*: "The world is full
of infinite causes that were never experienced before". All
too true: the tarpon have gone.

But once in a while a fish strikes. Amid a whoosh of
surface foam, a giant mouth like a silver bucket opens
and sucks the fly in. You strike back immediately, and
whip the fly right out of the tarpon's mouth. Or you wait
a second, strike, and connect. Just as you might put the
cast right one time in three, and the fish might take the
fly one time in five, so you might, with luck, get one hook-
up in three strikes. The odds thus far are not great: one in
45, and this is before the tarpon has even begun to fight.

They have jaws like concrete blocks, solid bone and
gristle. Probably the hook will not hold. But if it does,
both you and the tarpon are in trouble – you more than it.
You realise this when the fish begins its run, and the slack
line that had been lying on the carpeted foredeck hits the
first rod guide in a knot. You claw it loose. It sizzles out,
and suddenly the fish is on the reel. You are now attached
to a creature of extraordinary strength and wildness, which
tears all the fly-line off the reel in a matter of seconds,
and will be 100 metres into the backing before you can
recover your breath. It is common for a biggish tarpon – 30
kilograms or more – to run for a few kilometres in long
dashes before it is brought to boat (*if* it is), so the guide has
no choice but to cast off from the pole and follow it around
the flats. Its predicament, basically, is that it can run but not

hide. The flats are shallow, rarely more than a couple of metres deep, so the tarpon cannot sound, and they contain no structure, such as rocks or wrecks or reefs, in which it can hole up and break the line. Since it cannot go down, it goes up, repeatedly. The jump of a tarpon is startling and scary. It can go as high as three metres. The fish explodes out of the water, twisting and whipping, a column of quicksilver in a storm of foam. It is an epiphany. Nothing is more silver than a tarpon in the sunlit air. It hangs at the top of its arc and then crashes back into the sea. Then it does it again, and again. Short of a big billfish tail-walking, these acrobatics are the most exhilarating sight that fishing affords. If the leader doesn't snap or the hook pull out of the fish's mouth after these jumps, you probably have a good chance of getting the tarpon in. But it is a slugging fight all the way, and after the first half-hour your rod arm begins to burn as though you've been chopping mahogany with a tomahawk. If you do wear the tarpon down to the point where it comes alongside, and then release it, the relief is mutual. It would be absurd to kill it; better to be left with nothing but a photograph of its gleaming, ancient head and your beetroot-coloured face. Do not, above all, think of having its corpse mounted as a trophy. Fish taxidermy is a steady business in Florida, but when you deliver your tarpon it won't come back stuffed. The real fish will be weighed, measured, and then ignominiously tossed in a rubbish skip. You will receive, for many, many dollars more, a generic fibreglass tarpon, which are made as blanks in incremental sizes, airbrushed to silvery lifelikeness, and kept in storage by the taxidermist until some deluded angler brings in a fish of the right size. It would have been better to short-circuit the whole business and buy one direct from Friendly Freddy the Fish Stuffer. Some cheats do this. I used to know an art collector with a giant battleship of a house perched on the dunes at Easthampton. Over his fireplace hung a body mould of a billfish, purchased at a garage sale. Cannily, he neither claimed nor denied catching it. His non-fishing guests assumed the former; his fishing guests, who knew he wasn't a fisherman, thought it was by Damien Hirst or Jeff Koons. It was perfect: a postmodernist, virtual trophy of a combat that never happened, an ironic gloss on the importance of being Ernest Hemingway.

II

FRESH WATER

UNLIKELY AS IT MAY SEEM, MY FIRST IDENTIFIABLY sexual memories are associated with fish and fishing. Back in 1950, when I was eleven years old, I came across a book in my father's library: *Salar the Salmon*, by Henry Williamson. This short and elaborately written book is sometimes referred to as an "angling classic" – but actually it isn't about angling at all, at least not from the viewpoint of the angler. It is about life underwater, into which human enemies sometimes intrude; it is a novel whose central character is an Atlantic salmon, ascending its home stream to spawn after its long migration. It is pre-Disney, in that it contains no trace of the pathologically sentimental grafting of human characteristics into non-human creatures that has overrun the childish imagination since Bambi, the fawn with no anus, first hit the silver screen. In its depiction of the Darwinian world in which sea creatures actually live, where everything is prey to everything else, it seemed alien and utterly fascinating. At the end of his odyssey, having run the gauntlet of seals, otters, nets and a villainous lamprey, Salar finally reaches his biological Ithaca: the spawning beds, or "redds". There, a hen salmon named Gralaks – "ripe, ready to drop her eggs" – is scooping a trough in the gravel to spawn in. Salar moves in on her. "She jerked and shook on her side, as though trying to touch the back of her neck with her tail. Eggs dribbled quickly from her . . . [Salar] moved forward, feeling as though he were being drawn from underneath by a lamprey of sweeter and sweeter sensation. His milt flowed from him in a mist . . . For a few moments Salar lay in ecstasy on the redd." And, lucky devil, he just keeps going.

> As the days went on Salar became heavy with weariness. Most of his milt was shed; in slow pulse after slow pulse his life's sweetness had been drawn from him, leaving with each emptiness a greater inflaming desire, which during the day lapped about the wasted body with dreams of an everlasting sea of rest; but when darkness came, and the water was ashine with stars, he felt himself running bright with the river, and sweetness returned to him on the redd beside Gralaks.

Phew. A tad overwrought, you may think, though I didn't at the time. A flagrant bit of RBP (rich, beautiful prose) it may be, though not inherently sillier than the sex scenes in *Lady Chatterley's Lover*, which of course I had never even heard of. Perhaps you had to be there – a

pre-teenager with unidentified longings beginning to stir
in him, in a family and a culture that were single-mindedly
bent on maintaining his purity for as long as possible.
In Australia in 1950 there were no sex manuals, no maga-
zines full of naked girls with staples in their navels, no
novels with "explicit" passages. Even less could you down-
load, from the Web, pictures of alleged schoolgirls doing
weird things with enormously well-endowed ponies. Such
improvements were far in the future. The strictest censor-
ship reigned in civil life, and in Catholic life it was even
stricter. One was meant to confess one's "impure thoughts"
to the priest, but this I never did. Somehow it just seemed
too complicated to explain to Monsignor O'Regan, in the
dark and stuffy confines of the confessional booth of Saint
Mary Magdalen's at Rose Bay, how I had been led to them
by a description of spawning fish. He might have thought
I was some kind of pervert in the making, not just an
ordinary prepubescent sinner. It was one thing to risk the
fires of hell, but quite another to look like a fool. Besides
which, although Henry Williamson had told me what fish
got up to, I was still far from clear about what people did.

The other memory comes from 1952, the year after my
father died, when I was thirteen. Gradually the clutter of
stuff he left behind him in cupboards and drawers had
been winnowed out: rods and guns going to my elder
brothers, clothes sent to Catholic charities. But a lot of
small things remained, and since nobody wanted to throw
them away, I would sometimes paw circumspectly through
the contents of the drawers, trying to recover some detail

or other of the life of a man whom I deeply loved but
now would never know as an adult. It was in this way
that I came across the first visual image of a semi-naked
woman that I had ever seen. It was not a photograph. It
was moulded, in clear perspex, on the spool on which an
American fly-fishing line had been coiled. The brand
name was Rain-Beau, a pun in Art Deco lettering. I forget
the manufacturer's name. It had been made in some place
called Milwaukee, far away in unimaginable America.
Lucky Americans, to have such things on their fishing
gear! The scene was a river, with perspex eddies flowing
past perspex rocks. Smack in the centre, next to a rock,
was the girl. Her actual height was perhaps five centimetres, but she looked willowy and, I was sure, tall. A mane
of hair cascaded down her back, coiling like the eddies
in the water. Though it was perspex, I was convinced she
was blond. She was fly-fishing. Her rod was bent in an arc
under the pull of a trout, which could be seen leaping.
Her backside and legs were hidden, although suggestively,
in waders. But you could see her bare back and, most
important, the profile of her breast. It was perky and, as
such dimensions go in five-centimetre-high girls, quite
large. I thought her mysterious and entrancing – a sexpot
nymph of the stream. (Indeed, from then on I could not
hear the word *nymph* uttered, as it often is by fly-fishers,
without thinking of her.) For sure, you never saw girls
like that on Rose Bay pier, only other scrubby small boys
with freckles, rugby scabs, and hand lines, along with a
few old codgers on the dole. Unconsciously, I suppose, I

thought of her as a reward of the more refined and difficult kind of fishing that had begun to invade my imagination: fishing with a fly in rivers, not with bait in the sea.

For by then I was deep into fly-fishing, more in theory than in everyday practice, since there were no trout-bearing rivers near Sydney. My father had been a keen fly-fisherman, and so were my elder brothers. He was a strict purist when it came to any sport, but particularly about shooting and fishing. *Assume that any gun you touch is loaded. Never point it at anything you don't intend to shoot at. Never shoot anything alive unless you mean to eat it. And never, under any circumstances, fish for trout with anything but a fly.*

This prohibition had both practical and moral aspects. The practical one was that fly-fishing was usually a more effective way to catch trout than live-baiting. You could, indeed must, figure out what they were feeding on and then choose a fly to match the food, whether that happened to be larvae on the stream bottom, smaller fish, or insects descending on the water. Your fly-box, with its wide palette of different patterns, gave you the means to do this more efficiently, and of course more elegantly, than barging around on the riverbank catching beetles in your hat. The moral aspect was related to the elegance.

From the time I was seven or eight, after my father had been released from service as a flying instructor in the Royal Air Force, the whole family – or as much of it as could be assembled – would go camping together on the Murrumbidgee River, in a valley named Yaouk, near Jindabyne, almost 500 kilometres south of Sydney, in the foothills of the Australian Alps. The tent – a many-roomed structure of heavy canvas, with a bewildering array of poles, pegs and guy-ropes – would be packed into a two-wheeled trailer, along with the rest of the gear: grill, bush oven, kerosene lamps, Primus stove, cooking utensils, a folding table and chairs, rod cases, a pair of shotguns, a .22 single-shot rifle, duffel bags of clothes, food, books and the Thunderbox, a folding single-hole wooden lavatory seat. The Hughes clan did not travel light, and this mass of stuff, tarped over and roped down, rose quite high above the sides of the trailer. It was as if we were heading for Africa, though without native bearers. The whole shebang was then hitched to the family car, a turtle-like machine called a Chrysler Airflow. We would pack ourselves in and set off. Due to the primitive state of Australian roads then, the trip would take ten hours, evening to breakfast time, with occasional stops for car-sickness. But it was worth it. One arrived in the dry crackling paradise of the Australian bush: a golden valley, resonant with bird calls, through which the Murrumbidgee flowed gin-clear over its pebbled bed, with backwaters full of undisturbed wild duck. It took all morning to unpack and raise the tent, and then there was lunch, but by afternoon we'd be free to fish.

Not that I was – at first. At nine I was not old and responsible enough to have a trout rod of my own. These rods were precious and, in post-war Australia, irreplaceable. They were exquisitely slender, three-piece split-cane rods, handmade before the war by the London firm, Hardy. The days of the mass-produced fibreglass or, later,

boron-graphite fly-rod were far in the future. Cane rods were inordinately prone to damage, and a whole etiquette of handling attached to them. You couldn't lay one on the ground, in case you stepped on it and broke it. You had to lean it up against a tree, always vertical. Walking to the river, you had to carry the rod in three pieces, never assembled, so as not to run the tip into a bush and bust it. And so on and so forth; a samurai in dealing with his sword could hardly have been more circumscribed by ritual usage. The first year I went to Yaouk I was not allowed to touch the rods, though I would do so, surreptitiously, marvelling at their lightness and finesse. The second year I was allowed to practise casting, always under adult supervision. Not until my third visit there was I turned loose on the water, on my own. The result was not good.

I can see the pool still, of course. A kilometre upstream from camp, with perfect solitude and a silence broken only by a crow saying at intervals, as Australian crows morosely do, *fark*. A few metres wide, glass-clear, with deep dark overhangs. In the middle, several rocks. And behind each of them, hanging in the eddy, a trout, just like the ones I had studied in the river before and scrutinised in the diagrams of my various trout books. Except that now I had a rod and some flies. All over the pool, fish were rising, not just dimpling the surface with demure rings, but slashing at the grasshoppers falling into the stream. The air was alive with grasshoppers. All thumbs, I managed to tie a fly to my leader. The first clumsy cast snagged me in a bush.

The second, in a gum tree. The third landed in a dog's breakfast of tangles on the water. The fourth, likewise. It was a nightmare. And when I finally got some semblance of rhythm into my casting, the trout ignored the flies, which didn't look like grasshoppers. This went on for half an hour, maybe more. Finally, sweating with frustration, I decided to break the great taboo. I got out my pocketknife, scraped the feathers off the largest fly I had, knotted the bare hook on, and impaled a fat, kicking hopper on it. Then I flipped it into the water. It floated, struggling, past the nearest rock. Instantly there was a swirl and, for the first time in my life, I was connected to a trout, and through it to the rest of the universe. It wasn't a giant – a brown, maybe a kilogram in size – but it fought like a Kilkenny cat, making long, erratic runs and jumping into the air to show its golden spotted flanks. I did everything right. I dipped the rod tip when it jumped. I didn't freeze on the reel when it ran. I led sideways to tire the fish more. I knew what it was going to do and saw everything it did. I was in ecstasy. And at last, having fumbled the landing net from the hook on my belt, I was floating the exhausted fish into the mesh when the voice of Jehovah fell on me, like a ton of bricks, from the sky.

"Let that fish go!" it commanded.

I straightened up and looked wildly about me. Nothing. Then, to my horror, the head and chest of my father rose into view from where he had been watching everything I did, behind a big fallen eucalyptus trunk on the far bank.

"Release that fish!" he boomed.

I twisted the hook from its jaw and watched it half drift, half swim away downstream.

"Now come over here."

Filled with foreboding, I waded across the pool. I noticed, with worse foreboding, that Dad had unbuckled his belt and was pulling it out of the loops. He gently took the rod from my hand, leant it carefully against the fallen trunk, and then less gently seized my arm, spun me around, and delivered a slashing stroke of the belt to my backside. It didn't hurt much.

"I saw that", he said grimly. "You got that trout with a hopper. You will never do that again. People who use live bait on trout are not fit to fish. They are thugs. They are barbarians. They might as well be using dynamite. Now, get back to camp."

Snivelling, hot with shame, I followed him. I was allowed back on the river the next day, and I have never since fished for trout with anything but an artificial fly. Perhaps in some spirit of expiation toward the god of fishing purity, I began to transfer the hobby mania that kids are apt to have away from building model aircraft and on to the tying of trout flies. There were copious examples at home, together with pattern books and the gear you needed to make flies: a tiny vise with pointed jaws to hold the hooks, forceps, thread, wax, varnish to seal the final knot behind the hook's eye, and dozens of small cellophane envelopes containing feathers. I turned them out by the score, perky confections of fluff and hackle that, for all I knew, had no similarity to Australian insects. But the ritual:

that was what mattered. And sometimes they worked. The first time I caught a trout on a fly of my own making was on a stream called Spencers Creek, a tributary of the Snowy River that flowed down a bony, bare hillside near Mount Kosciusko, the highest peak in Australia. I remember the near-abstract perfection of that stream: no entangling bushes, just big ledges of elephant-grey rock, snow-worn into gentle voluminous curves with sudden facets where the boulders had broken off, with the hillside mantled in wiry flattened grass and snow daisies rising out of the water. I was thirteen and fishing on my own, having walked a long way in from the road. There was a pool, maybe 100 metres long, clear as green glass. I looked down on it from a smooth spur of granite. And there, hovering behind a large sunken rock, was a big trout. These elements – fish, rock, water, landscape – came together with astounding clarity, and I felt like their possessor. To complete the circle I must catch the fish with a fly I had tied myself, and no other would do. I picked out a March Brown, knotted it to the leader, and made one cast. I felt what tennis players or golfers do when the stroke is as sweet as it can be. The line shot out with a slight upstream curve; the leader turned over just as the books said it should; the fly parachuted softly onto the water, the transparent current bore it past the rock, and the fish rose to it. Fifteen minutes later I had him on the bank: a deep-bodied rainbow. I made a fire of snowgum twigs and, when it had burned down, roasted him in the embers for lunch. The charred skin and scales came clean away, and his flesh was a deep pink from his diet of crayfish. I ate every scrap of him. I had never tasted anything as delicious, or as sacramental. Later, on the way back to the road, it occurred to me that I had at last done something, in relation to fish, of which my father would have fully approved. But he was dead, and beyond approving anything.

That fixed belief in the superiority of fly-fishing for trout over all other ways of angling, held by my father and so many others like him – where did it come from? Evidently, class. It hardly existed before the English, in the nineteenth century, turned it into a mystique. Then it spread from England to America, and to the rest of the European-based world.

The earliest known reference to fly-fishing occurs in *De Natura Animalium* (On the Nature of Animals) by Aelian, a Roman writer of the late second and early third centuries A.D., who described how it was done by Macedonians on a river called the Astraeus. The fish in question may or may not have been trout, but they were partial to a large insect locally known as a *hippurus*, resembling a bumble-bee but useless as bait because its delicate wings shrivelled at human touch. So the cunning Macedonians "wrap the hook in scarlet wool, and to the wool they attach two feathers that grow beneath a cock's wattles and are the colour of wax" – producing a beelike, furry-bodied fly with wings. This, Aelian says, deceived the fish every time. He makes no claim that this was a "nobler" way of catching fish, only that it worked. There was no noble way of taking fish, because fish themselves weren't noble. Their pursuit was an entirely plebeian occupation.

Hunting was noble, the sport of kings and of gods. It was a means of transcendence. You proved your heroism, your fitness to command, by going up against, say, a wild boar in the woods of Thessaly with a spear. The ancient world assigned no imputation of bravery to catching mullet. Compared to the body of myth and legend that gathered around hunting, the ancient symbolism of fishing was quite meagre.

This would change with the coming of Christianity. But it remains a mystery why the fish became a Christian symbol. Its precedents were slight. The Syrians, for instance, had a religious respect for fish that, according to Xenophon (*Anabasis* 1.4.9) impressed the Greeks; the ritual sacrifice of fish was not uncommon in the ancient world, and in particular it was part of Roman ceremonies of appeasement of the early fire god Vulcan. In the summer, the hottest part of the year, live fish taken from the Tiber would be thrown into a fire. This offering to Vulcan of wet creatures normally safe from his doings must have been meant to induce him to spare his natural prey, like summer crops or the dry structure of houses. But there was no fish god, or god who was part fish, in the Roman or Greek pantheons, though of course the sea had its own deities, starting with the Greek Poseidon (known to the Romans as Neptune).

To the Roman nobs, fishing was bucolic and uninteresting, and fishermen belonged with shepherds, labourers and

peasants, just above slaves. To the literate and influential, these people were so far down the social scale that they were not fully human and could be made into an amusing, "instructive" spectacle: illiterate, scarred by age and work, figures in an idyll. They could be scanned with an appreciative eye, but without the slightest fellow feeling, becoming the subject of genre sculpture for the patrician arcade or garden: the old fisherman carrying his creel, with withered flesh and ropey muscles, was a common type, and one such sculpture, in the collection of the Vatican Museums, was wrongly supposed for many years to represent the aged Seneca. This philosopher-dramatist, who preached moderation but accumulated a huge fortune in his hypocritical greed and toadying to the Imperial Court, would not have been pleased to be taken for a prole.

In the ancient world and the early Christian era, practically no one seems to have fished for pleasure. The ancient Romans were big fish eaters, and the more extravagant among them laid out huge sums on private fish ponds. However, the only ancient Roman – certainly the only powerful one – known to have fished for sport was Mark Antony, who, according to Plutarch, went angling in the harbour of Alexandria with Cleopatra, and cheated at it: he paid some local fishermen in advance to dive under their barge and snag live fish on his hook, so as to cut a *bella figura* in front of his temptress. Cleopatra, once she caught on, paid him back by having her own slaves sneak down into the water and impale a salted fish on Antony's hook, much to the glee of the courtiers. And this pretence of fishing, to judge from Plutarch's account, was part of a pattern of social transvestism the two lovers enjoyed – they would also go slumming incognito late at night, getting into scrapes with the lower classes.

"Piso's a Christian, he worships a fish / There'd be no kissing if he had his wish", complains W. H. Auden's line soldier, scratching his lice on Hadrian's Wall. Probably the early Christian identification of Jesus Christ with a fish (in Greek, *ichthys*) came – like Christianity itself – from the Middle East rather than Rome. It was made more popular and memorable among early converts by becoming an acronym for their coded profession of faith: I [esos] Ch [ristos] Th [eou] U [ios] S [oter] – "Jesus Christ, son of God, Saviour". Perhaps the image of the fish, elusive and slippery, also suited a clandestine religious cult persecuted by authority.

But Christ and his first followers, as readers of the Bible well know, weren't just fish but fishermen. Four of the Apostles (Andrew, James, John and of course Peter) were busy at the tedious work of net mending by the Sea of Galilee when Christ recruited them by offering to make them "fishers of men"; from then on, the image of the evangelist fishing for souls would proliferate throughout the religious imagery of the West. It had strong plebeian associations. Fishing was work – hard, sometimes danger-ous, uncertain in its returns, meagre in its profits. Almost all of it was done with nets. Hence the fishing net, for Christians, became identified with virtuous labour. Nets were honest; they did not deceive the fish. You dragged them through the water, but they didn't lure the prey into them. This was an important symbolic point when it came to depicting the various Christianised forms of fishing. Souls were swept up, gathered in the net of doctrine and faith. That they were all together in the net symbolised the community of the Church. That fish swam into the net of their own accord chimed with the Catholic doctrine of free will, of voluntary acceptance of the gospel truth. "In this Sea", preached John Donne, in a sermon he gave in St Paul's in 1619,

> are we made fishers of men: of Men in generall: not of rich men, to profit by them, nor of poore men, to pierce them the more sharply, because affliction hath opened a way into them; Not of learned men, to be over-glad of their approbation of our labours, Nor of ignorant men, to affect them with an aston-ishment, or an admiration of our gifts; But we are fishers of men, of all men, of that which makes them men, their souls. And for this fishing in this Sea, this Gospel is our net.

Any means of catching the soul other than the direct and all-inclusive, net-like word of God must verge on the diabolic: "Eloquence is not our net: Traditions of men are not our nets; only the Gospel is." But angling, fishing with a rod and line and bait – that was a different matter. It entailed deception and guile in that the hook was hidden; the angler was archetypally a liar. "The Devil angles with hooks and bayts; he deceives, and he wounds in the catching; for every sin hath his sting."

For this reason, neither Christ nor any of his Apostles was ever depicted "fishing for men" with a rod and line. The only exceptions to this were mediaeval images of God the Father angling for Leviathan, using Christ as bait and the cross as a hook. But that was fair, since Leviathan, the sea monster of the Nile, was by then fused with the image of Satan, himself the father of lies, and one could kill a liar by cunning, using Satan's own wiles to defeat him.

There was no such moral contrast between net and hook in the East, and in both China and Japan fishing was considered a worthy relaxation for scholars, courtiers and aristocrats long before it became so in Europe. Japanese nobles of the Momoyama period built ornamented pavilions by their ponds, so that they could fish for carp. Chinese ink paintings depicted sages thinking, presumably, of philosophical matters while dangling a hair-thin line in the water. Verses extolled the freedom from mundane worries implied by fishing, and some, like Po Chu-I in 811 A.D., even said it didn't matter whether one caught a fish or not.

> I, when I have come to cast my hook in the stream,
> Have no thought of either fish or men.
> Lacking the skill to capture either prey
> I can only bask in the autumn water's light.
> When I tire of this, my fishing also stops;
> I go to my home and drink my cup of wine.

Perhaps because fishing in China was a high-class sport as well as common work, Chinese anglers were far ahead of

European techniques. In Europe, angling with a rod and line had been practised since about 300 B.C. But the line was fixed to the rod, whose length determined the scope of the angler's throw. Playing a fish by letting it take line and then recovering it was unknown. You had to depend on the springiness of the rod and the strength of the line. Izaak Walton claimed that the best strategy with a strong-running fish on a fixed line was to toss the rod into the water and let the fish drag it around until it tired. This is palpable nonsense, and not even his disciple Charles Cotton believed it. Long before, the inventive Chinese came up with a better idea: the fishing reel, wound with a running line. Probably it developed out of silk technology: Joseph Needham, the great scholar of Chinese science, speculated that someone had the bright idea of adapting a winding bobbin to use as a small winch. But whatever their origins, unmistakable fishing reels, attached to rods fitted with line guides, were turning up in Chinese paintings by the thirteenth century A.D. Not until the mid-seventeenth century do they appear in England. The first English writer to mention a reel was Thomas Barker, in *The Art of Angling* (1651); two years later Walton, a garrulous giver of technical advice, mentions that some salmon fishers "use a wheel about the middle of their rod, or near their hand, which is to be observed better by seeing one of them, than by a large demonstration of words".

The West, too, was slower to grasp the possibilities of fishing as something other than work – as a pastime, a mode of contemplation, or (as the subtitle to Walton's

The Compleat Angler puts it) "the contemplative man's recreation".

The first piece of Western writing to enshrine this idea is in the *Book of St Albans*, printed at Westminster in 1496 by the aptly named publisher Wynkyn de Worde. It is an essay titled "A Treatyse of Fysshynge with an Angle". Its author is unknown; traditionally it was ascribed to a noblewoman who had become a nun, Dame Juliana Berners, but there seems to be no evidence that she actually wrote it, if indeed she existed at all. No matter: "A Treatyse" is the starting point of all fishing literature in English. It would be copied, quoted and plagiarised for the next 300 years (most notably by Izaak Walton in *The Compleat Angler*, the most frequently reprinted book of all time next to the Bible and *Pilgrim's Progress*, but also by such ponderous luminaries as Robert Burton in *The Anatomy of Melancholy*). Its basic message is that fishing is good for you, that it leads to health, long life and virtue. Not so with commercial netting, whose long hours in bad weather can be the source of "grete Infirmytees". The netman can lose his tackle and his money with it, but all an angler stands to lose is a line and a hook – and perhaps a fish, if it breaks off. This, the author says, is "not grievous". ("Depends on the fish", another angler might mutter.)

What "Dame Juliana" clearly admires is the modest self-sufficiency of the angler, compared to the showier and more elitist rituals of the Plantagenet hunter or falconer. The angler walks and looks, takes in the landscape and its creatures without disturbing either. "A sweet air of the sweet savour of the meadow flowers" – I am modernising the usage – "that makes him hungry. He hears the melodious harmony of birds. He sees the young swans, herons, ducks, coots and many other birds with their broods: which seems better to me than all the noise of hounds, the blast of horns . . . that hunters, falconers and fowlers can make." The angler must get up early, which, "Dame Juliana" optimistically thinks, "shall cause hym to be holy". Fishing is good for the body, too, and for one's material estate, "for it shall make hym riche". (There has never been any evidence that the last is true; the only people who have ever made a buck from amateur fishing are the makers of fishing gear, unless you include those impaired souls who lay bets on the outcome of a day's angling. As for holiness, I'd be the last to dispute the spiritual benefits of fishing, but it is also a great source of sin: taking the Lord's name in vain, filthy language, envy and above all, lying.)

These benefits imply duties. "Dame Juliana" was the first fishing writer in English to stress what we now call eco-responsibility and to sketch a code of behaviour for anglers. Don't trespass on any "poore mannes" pond or stream, don't disturb his fish traps – or heinous and unsporting thought – steal the fish from them, even if they're in common water. Close the gates behind you and try not to step on the eggs of waterfowl. Don't go fishing with a whole bunch of people, as their company will distract you from meditation and prayer. Above all, don't take more fish than you need, because that will ruin the sport for yourself and others. Such admonitions, like the warnings given in fifteenth-century etiquette books – don't spit on the floor during dinner, don't blow your nose on the napkin or pick it at the table – may tell us something about the actual state of fishing customs in late Gothic England. They still hold true. "Dame Juliana" was the mother superior of bag limits and catch-and-release conventions.

She also set a tone, which transmitted itself to later fishing writers – not that the genre got very big until the nineteenth century. Fishing didn't have the arrogance of "noble" hunting, and you didn't have to be rich to do it; all you needed was leisure, which connoted some independence of means, but certainly not the security of the landed gentry. (The poor did not hunt; they "poached," and were hanged or transported for it.) You might almost call it democratic, if democracy had existed in Izaak Walton's time. Its ultimate object was not to fill a bag with fish, but to acquire a closeness to Nature and a certain inner balance; "study to be quiet" was the motto of *The Compleat Angler*. Angling dissolved the long debate over whether the *vita activa* (the active life, that of the hero) or the *vita contemplativa* (the reflective one of the philosopher or anchorite) was better, because it was both. Angling was amateur, and it supplied a refined pleasure not to be had from netting, tickling, trapping, gaffing, stunning or poisoning fish. The mild Walton gets severe on those unsporting souls who go after trout at night with torches and spears: "This kind of way they catch very many: but I would not believe it till I was an eyewitness of it, nor do I like it now that I have seen it." His disciple Charles

Cotton, who added the section on fly-fishing to *The Compleat Angler*, is more forthright, inveighing against the ruin of rivers by "the basest sort of people, by those unlawful ways of fire and netting in the night, and of damming, groping, spearing, hanging and hooking by day! which are now grown so common, that, although we have very good laws to punish such offenders, every rascal does it." The angler does not sell his fish; he eats them with friends, or gives them away to passing milkmaids, who sing songs for him in exchange for their supper. "Marry, God requite you, Sir", effuses one of these pastoral nymphs in *The Compleat Angler*, on accepting a chub,

> and we'll eat it cheerfully; and if you come this way a-fishing two months hence, a-grace of God I'll give you a syllabub of new verjuice in a new-made hay-cock for it, and my Maudlin shall sing you one of her best ballads; for she and I both love all Anglers, they be such honest, civil, quiet men.

She then warbles a song by Christopher Marlowe, "Come live with me, and be my love." It isn't exactly social realism, but never mind. What Walton is creating is a conventional idyll set in an English Eden. He is following, naturally enough for a man of his time and education, in the footsteps not only of "Dame Juliana" but of ancient Roman writers singing the blessings of the contemplative life in rural retreat, *procul negotiis, ut prisca gens mortalium*, in Horace's words – "far from business worries, like the first race of mortals". He bridles at the idea, held by some desensitised souls, that fishermen are nitwits. No, no, sir, the boot is on the other foot, Piscator the fisher tells Auceps the falconer:

> And for you that have heard many grave, serious men pity Anglers, let me tell you, Sir, there be many men that are by others taken to be serious and grave men, which we contemn and pity. Men that are taken to be grave, because nature hath made them of a sour complexion, money-getting men, – men that spend all their time first in getting, then in anxious care to keep it; men that are condemned to be rich, and then always busy or discontented; for these poor-rich-men, we Anglers pity them perfectly . . . No, no, Sir, we enjoy a contentedness above the reach of such dispositions.

Not only did Walton like an idyll, but, as Howell Raines points out in his introduction to a recent edition of *The Compleat Angler*, he needed one. As a loyal monarchist, he had fled from London into rural seclusion in 1643–44, when Cromwell and the Puritans began to get the upper hand, and his "appreciation of the pastoral beauties of the streamside and the milkmaid's sweet songs was no doubt sharpened by the fact that . . . [he] was sticking hooks into worms rather than having his own head displayed on the end of a New Model Army pike".

But Walton's idyll did not have a hierarchy of prey. Walton would as soon have taken a decent-size tench as any salmon or trout. The segregation of "coarse" fish, from the tiny bleak, gudgeon or stickleback on up to the obese carp, and their consignment to lower-class sport, had not yet begun. Nor had the corresponding elevation of trout and salmon. But one sees it beginning in Cotton's post-script to *The Compleat Angler*: "Doubtless, a Trout affords the most pleasure to the Angler of any sort of fish what-ever; and the best Trouts must needs make the best sport." Still, until the beginning of the nineteenth century salmon were among the commonest of English fish, and cheap, too: workers and labourers would complain if they were given them to eat too often, and the same applied to oysters, which in Samuel Pepys's day cost pennies a barrel. (On the same principle, English line soldiers in the Crimean War bitterly resented being issued rations of a black, fishy, granular jam in place of their regular bully beef. It was caviar.)

Just how the salmonids – trout, salmon, char, grayling and their various relatives – came to be regarded as aristocratic game fish and the numerous other freshwater species as coarse is an interesting question with no simple answer, but no sociologist (or none that I can find) seems to have gone deeply into it. The discrimination began in the late eighteenth century and had become fixed in England by the mid-nineteenth. My own guess – perhaps a rather obvious one – is that it descended from the intense concern with property laws in Georgian England. Stable property, and the absolute right to control public access to it, was one of the prime clear signs of social stability for a landowning class that often felt threatened from below by

agrarian unrest. One of the highest marks of a desirable
landholding was that, to use a much later phrase, "a river
runs through it", and that this river should hold fish,
whose safety from proletarian intrusion must be upheld by
law. Georgian England witnessed a continuous struggle
between fish poachers and fish owners, spurred not so
much by the economic importance of the fish to the
landowner as by its symbolic value. The monster of all
property acts, the Waltham Black Act of 1722, was passed in
response to some minor agrarian uprisings in Hampshire,
and it prescribed the gallows for some 200 different
offences to property, including the theft of live fish from
streams and ponds – this at a time when attempted murder
of live humans was still classed only as a misdemeanor. In
English social portraiture, the creel of freshly caught trout
joined the game bag of dead fur and feathers as one of
the marks of the gentleman, at ease in his acres.

As the English countryside was transformed by the
Industrial Revolution, both the old landed gentry and
the new mercantile one whose coal mines and iron works
were fouling the streams and blackening the meadows of
an earlier England naturally wanted to have their own
unpolluted crystal rills, the image of whose purity was
the trout. It was an Arcadian fish, which could only live
in clear running water, unlike the lowly tench or carp,
which could stand any amount of mud and gunk. Its
flesh was firm and delicious. It looked supremely elegant,
with its quicksilver flanks and rosy speckles. Its proportions
were refined and its presence mild and elusive (the grayling

was also called an umber, from *umbra*, Latin for "shadow").
Trout were fastidious. They spooked easily, thus summon-
ing from the fisherman his reserves of those gentlemanly
qualities, delicacy and circumspection. To fish "fine and
far" (with a light leader, standing well back and making
a long cast) was first enjoined by Cotton as a practical
technique; by the nineteenth century it had become a
stylistic imperative, a sign of class, like keeping a straight
bat at cricket, which was also in those days a gentleman's
sport. Trout fought bravely but surrendered gracefully.
Once in hand, they could not jag you with spines, cut
you with their gill covers, or inflict bites with their teeth.
Nor were they covered with thick slime. The gear of fly-
fishing was clean, minimal. One handled a neat little tuft of
feathers. One did not have to bother with the sometimes
noisome baits used for coarse fish: slimy minnows, smelly
pastes, the "ground-bait" or chum, or especially the pallid
maggots, known euphemistically as "gentles", associated
with corruption and the grave. (You wouldn't want to know
what went into some of those compound baits. One seven-
teenth-century recipe included human fat and powdered
bones, "mummy", cat fat, and grave earth – everything but
a Tartar's lips and the liver of a blaspheming Jew.)

The whole iconography of trout fishing befitted a
gentleman – that is, a person of independent income,
preferably landed, with ample leisure and a calm, philosophical disposition. Such a man, wrote James Saunders in
The Compleat Fisherman (1724), "must have all his Passions
at his Command, he must govern his Temper with an

absolute Sway, and be able to sustain his Mind under the greatest Disappointments". In sum, he ought not stamp on his rods in frustration, curse and swear, or – as one particularly gross media mogul did in the presence of a friend of mine in Alaska a few years ago – yank out a hogleg .44 Magnum and blow to shreds a landed salmon in pettish rage at being told he must release it. The true gentleman angler could not, by Saunders's reckoning, be a "Man of Business", because if he left his counting house to go fishing he "makes the Sport become a Vice in his Morals; his Angling is a Crime". Nor should he make fishing into a business, which lowered its tone. Such assumptions permeated the English literature of angling, which grew large through the nineteenth century and into the twentieth. Not only was the artificial fly better than natural bait, but the dry fly, which floated on the surface of the water, was morally superior to the wet fly, which did not; and both had a stylistic edge over the nymph, which had no wings and drifted along the bottom, emulating the larval stage of the insect. To catch a trout on a tiny fly, tied on a #16 or even #18 hook attached to a leader of gossamer thinness, was clearly a more elegant achievement than getting one on larger tackle. In due course, the whole Victorian-Edwardian Bushido of fine-tackle, dry-fly fishing would migrate from the chalk streams of Kent to the rivers of America, where it grew enormously. The chief transmitter of this fanaticism was an Englishman, Frederic M. Halford, whose bizarrely snobbish book *Dry-Fly Fishing in Theory and Practice* (1889) won numerous converts in the United States. Though they got rid of Lord North and George III long ago, Americans are ravenous for Anglo-derived signs of style, and large businesses, such as Ralph Lauren's fashion empire, have been raised on packaging these fictions to eager customers. Hence the annual appearance on the rivers of New England, such as the Battenkill, of dedicated anglers wielding implausibly fragile two-weight rods, preferably made of old-fashioned bamboo rather than state-of-the-art synthetics. With these they "present" (the verb, with its ceremonious aura, is significant) diminutive flies to trout rarely more than half a kilogram in weight – fish so jaded from being caught and released that they can tell an Orvis-tied Grey Wulff or Rat-Faced McDougal from a homemade one. In the country of gorge-and-puke consumption, the catch-and-release angler rejoices in his ethical apartness. And quite right, too, because if American anglers killed the trout they caught, there would soon be no trout left.

Catch-and-release, apart from its virtues in preserving the fish population, is the liar's friend: all trout grow when you let them go. Most fly-fishers lie, but they do not compete. Or to put it more precisely, there are no frames within which they *can* compete. For "coarse" freshwater anglers, there are.

The fishing tournament, American style, is a wildly mutated descendant of local competitions that developed among English coarse-fishers generations ago. As trout and salmon streams were closed to the hoi polloi in the nineteenth century, other opportunities to fish appeared.

The Industrial Revolution changed fishing, along with everything else in England. It brought a great increase of sport fishing among ordinary working people. An ever-expanding railway network put thousands of folk within reach of canals, ponds and flooded quarry pits that were the by-products of industry. "Coarse" fish swam in them: pike and carp, tench and bream, and so on down to the tiny dace and gudgeon. The tackle for catching them evolved in a different direction to that of fly anglers: rods became immensely long, lines were often fixed rather than wound on a reel. Coarse-fishing clubs and societies proliferated. So did customs peculiar to the sport, such as the fishing tournament, a thing unheard of among trout fishermen but very popular at this democratic level. A strict practice of catch-and-release came to prevail. Since there was little point in distinguishing between one fish that weighed 85 grams and another of 90 grams, the prize tended to go to the biggest aggregate weight of fish – kept alive, weighed at the end of the day, and then released unharmed. No less than the fly-fishers, the coarse-anglers grew acutely aware of the need for conservation, without which their sport would disappear.

The most elaborate form of this impulse today is the freshwater bass-fishing tournament. It combines things that would have been as incomprehensible to earlier twentieth-century fishermen as to Izaak Walton: the private sport turns aggressively public, the contemplative craft becomes a competitive spectacle, an exhibition. It seems to be an iron law of American life that this always

happens to sports and pastimes. Even baseball began as
a long, pastoral game without showbiz overtones. As
Neil Gabler reminds us in his book *Life, the Movie*, its
changes were forced by "trying to survive in a twentieth-
century entertainment society that prized fast, hyper
and sensational . . . The new sports of choice were football
and basketball, which were better suited to the aesthetics
of television and to the ever-growing demand for bigger,
faster, louder that was the entertainment equivalent of a
new drug high." One could hardly credit that much excitement could be whipped up by the sight of people trying
to catch smallmouth bass, but one would, apparently,
be wrong. It all depends on how you get to the target
audience. If American know-how can put men on the
moon, it can turn bassing into a spectator sport.

Bass, both largemouth (*Micropterus salmoides*) and smallmouth (*M. dolomieu*), are God's chief gift to the American
freshwater angler. They live in ponds, lakes, swamps,
bayous, canals and river deltas all over the United States
and seem impervious to environmental miseries that
would put most other fish out of commission. They eat
voraciously, breed copiously, and fight hard for their size,
which rarely goes above three kilograms. They are acces-
sible to any kid who can get near fresh water. For many
Americans they are democracy with fins, up there in the
national pantheon with Big Macs, Old Glory and family
values. Since they will eat anything short of a Marlboro
butt, they sustain an industry of lure makers, all of them
turning out creepers, poppers, Hoppy Frogs, surface plugs,

wigglers, wobblers, divers, jelly worms and other pseudo-critters in iridescent or fluorescent plastic, with or without sound effects. Then there are the special bass boats, with 225-horsepower outboards to blast them across the water and silent electric motors to creep up on bass habitat; the electronic fish finders; the live wells; the trucks and trailers; and all the other trimmings. No one could deny the bass its place in the economic mainstream.

Still and all, someone else catching a bass can be a boring sight, as anyone knows who has seen one of those cable TV programmes featuring phlegmatic good ol' boys reeling them in. (*Close-up of small, indignant fish.* PISCATOR I: "Ah thut he wuz a pahnd bigger thun thet, the way he fought." PISCATOR II: "Yup.") So how do you turn an inherently solitary sport into an all-American spectacle like a big league game or a rodeo?

The answer is the bass-fishing contest, whose acme is the annual BASS Masters Classic World Championship Tournament. You can't just roll up, register and compete in it, any more than you can in the US Open or at Wimbledon. Many are called, as the Good Book declares, but few are chosen. It is preceded by some 20 preliminary local fish-offs, from Lake Okeechobee in Florida to Lake Powell in Arizona. From the top-scoring fishermen in each (there are, as yet, no female pro bass-anglers), 45 win their invitations to the grand final, which is held in a different spot each year: Greensboro, North Carolina, in 1998, New Orleans in 1999. "45 heroes chasing their American dream", effuses a press release from *Bassmaster*, and they're not kidding.

The first prize is $100,000, plus considerable pickings in endorsements from scores of sponsors – not up there with Andre Agassi's earnings yet, but not to be sneezed at, either. In 1998 the heroes and their fans were treated to a "pre-weigh-in extravaganza complete with laser lights and a nationally recognised singer", the country-and-western star Mark Chesnutt. And to mark the start of the Kmart Kids Classic and Autograph Day, Sergeant Tom Weigos, a member of the US Golden Knights parachuting team stationed at Fort Bragg, executed a flawless parachute jump from 1,000 metres, carrying the Stars and Stripes, landing smack on the rear deck of a Ranger bass boat, where he picked up a rod and made the first cast of the competition. The 1999 event promises to be even more extreme, with daily weigh-ins held in the Louisiana Superdome and a nearby convention centre full of thousands of square metres of fishing equipment on display, while, in the mornings, the 45 bass heroes advance upon the water in full parade mode, each accompanied by a journalist. "The 45 identical Ranger bass boats," declares the promotional sheet,

> towed by 45 matching Chevy trucks, carry the Classic contenders to the launch ramp behind an early-morning police escort each fishing day. Spectators line the highway . . . to watch their heroes take to the water. Amid the click and whir of cameras and the cheers of fans, the anglers try to concentrate on such things as fishing patterns, strategy, lure selection and weather.

It can't be easy, thinking about fish through all those clicks and whirs and rah-rahs, still less with a scribbling hack making notes in the boat all day. But if Tiger Woods can focus under stress, so can a Bassmaster.

III

TROUBLED WATER

FISHING IS A CRUEL SPORT. ALL BLOOD SPORTS are, though that is not necessarily a reason for abolishing them. How would you like it if fish and angler were reversed? It is a bright, breezy May day and you are strolling along one of the piers at Malibu. You stop at a vendor's cart and buy a hot dog with mustard and relish. You lean on the railing and take a first bite. Suddenly your gullet is convulsed with a choking pain and a sharp pull snaps your head forward and down. Something hard, sharp and metallic is stuck in your throat. The shock is completely outside your experience. In an effort to resist it, you run frantically back and forth on the pier, but the pressure is inexorable, and your lungs have begun to fill with blood. Over the side you go, and hit the water wildly struggling. The unidentifiable force drags you down. On the bed of the bay, something enormous and unknown grabs you and, if you are lucky, kills you with a blow to the back of the head. If you are not so lucky, death comes more slowly by drowning. Either way, perhaps mercifully, you cannot hear or understand the Thing on the seabed chatting to its fellow Things about how well you fought.

This is more or less what happens to a hooked fish when it is pulled into a boat and left to suffocate. At one time or another, anglers have made all manner of dumb defences against the charge that their sport is cruel – typically, that fish don't feel pain as we do. This may or may not be true; all I can say, after 50 years of intermittent angling, is that if what they feel isn't pain, it is something so close to it as to make no difference. It may be that the hooked tarpon, with its rock-like mandibles undersupplied (by human standards) with nerves, feels no more in the course of the fight than you or I would at the dentist's. But because fish cannot communicate with us, or we with them, we do not know and never will. I have never known an angler who got pleasure from inflicting pain on a fish. Yet it defies reason to suppose that hooked fish do not suffer.

But reason is also defied by supposing that the angler, with his line and hook, is intruding into some kind of natural paradise – perhaps the octopus's garden of which the Beatles sang – where mermaids play and pain and violent death are unknown. Nothing that amateur anglers do to their prey even begins to rival in savagery what fish do to one another, or to other species. From the mayfly's point of view, the prettily speckled trout is a hellish monster. The coral polyp, if it knew dread, would dread the crunching jaws of the tropical wrasse. The bluefish

loves to kill beyond the bounds of its own appetite, and
will devour the young of its own species as impartially as
it will sand eels or menhaden. And let's not get started
on the dietary habits of the shark, the playful dolphin, or
Willie the Killer Whale. It's Murderland down there, high
tide or low, night and day. Fish have no ethics, only desires
and instincts.

In any case, the urgent question is not what individual
fish feel. Rather, it concerns the fate of entire species, and
of the oceans in which they swim. Hook-and-line anglers
have rarely had more than a marginal effect on fish populations. High-technology commercial fishing now does. 200
or even 100 years ago, fish were protected by the otherness
and impenetrability of the sea. Today they are menaced by
it. The sea's fauna are strip-mined, to an extent not imagin-
able a few human generations ago; the fishing industry
is devouring its own future. Those who oppose this find
themselves up against public incomprehension, because
most people can't imagine the sea as they can imagine the
land. Worse, they have difficulty entertaining the idea that
the sea and its contents are as essential to human life, both
physical and spiritual, as the land and the air. And yet,
97 per cent of our biosphere, the surface of our globe, is
ocean. "Every breath we take", wrote the marine biologist
Sylvia Earle, formerly the chief scientist of the National
Oceanic and Atmospheric Association,

is possible because of the life-filled, life-giving sea;
oxygen is generated there, carbon dioxide absorbed

. . . without the living ocean there would be no life
on land . . . the sea is Earth's life-support system.
The services provided are so fundamental that most
of us . . . take them for granted. In the past century,
without much thought about the consequences, we
have removed billions of tons of living creatures
from the sea and added to it billions of tons of toxic
substances. Fish, whales, shrimp, clams and other
living things are regarded as commodities, not as
vital components of a living system on which we
are utterly dependent.

From childhood, most Americans today are pumped full
of the image of Nature as a planet-sized petting zoo. Its
icons are benign, warm-blooded, air-breathing, and for
the most part mammalian: the dog, the cat, the rabbit,
the frisky lamb, the otter, the harp seal, the koala, the
lion, the bear and the tiger (preferably when they are
cubs), the panda and winsome Bambi. Almost all of them
are land-based. The only sea creatures on the list are
also air-breathing, viviparous mammals: the bottle-nosed
dolphin, *Tursiops truncatus*, with that built-in smile on its
snout, and of course the whales, great and small.

It is easy to have respect for creatures somewhat like
ourselves. The real test is to feel it for the immense major-
ity of species that are totally unlike us. Serious concern for
Nature must begin with a recognition of its otherness. The
"pathetic fallacy" – the habit of ascribing human emotions
and impulses to non-human entities – is to conservation

what a set of training wheels is to biking. It gets the
kiddies going, but it has to be left behind. Otherwise, bad
luck for the uncuddly, the non-feathered, the wet, the
cold-blooded and the myriad creatures that have more
than four legs or none at all.

Part of the difficulty in protecting fish, or at least in
regulating and reducing their wholesale killing, is their
utter unlikeness to us. They are not mammals, not warm-
blooded, not air-breathing, not "intelligent" (at least, not in
a way remotely perceptible to us); they are cold and dumb
and slimy, though often indubitably good to eat. They do
not seem emotional. They do not copulate and give birth
to their young. They have no conception of nurture: from
the instant a fish larva is out of its egg, it's on its own
among millions of others, most of which will die, not
infrequently gobbled up by members of their own species.

And they live in an environment that seems utterly alien
to ours, the watery planet whose surface most humans
never penetrate. We know less about the depths of the
sea than we know about the surface of Mars or the moon.
Our love for other species is highly selective, verging on a
sort of mammalian narcissism. The world's disappearing
fish populations are not going to be saved by impulses
based on sentiment or empathy, because *Homo sapiens*
have no more empathy for fish than fish do for us. When
the mad blonde played by Glenn Close in *Fatal Attraction*
boiled a pet rabbit, the audience was horrified. Few people
feel a similar revulsion when a lobster or a mud crab is
boiled alive. They just reach for the mayonnaise and dig

right in, as I do. Nobody cares much about the semi-feral cats that infest the Shelter Island rubbish dump, but if I were to go there at dawn with, say, a light spinning rod and half a frankfurter on a #6 hook to enjoy the thrill of playing one among the burst rubbish bags and junked TV sets until, exhausted and struggling weakly, it submitted to the net, to be released hurt but otherwise unharmed – in other words, if I treated an ownerless kitty the way millions of Americans treat the bass in their nearby ponds any day of the week – I would certainly be viewed by some neighbours as deeply eccentric and by others as not far removed from the hero of *The Silence of the Lambs*.

The fishing industry differs from all other food industries in that it is the only one based on the catching, killing and processing of wild animals. On the earth or in the air, the term "game" has become all but meaningless – it refers to creatures that were once hunted wild, but are now farmed. The venison you eat was not shot in the woods; it was raised on a farm, like any ordinary steer. Likewise the quail, the pheasant and the partridge are all raised like so many chickens, though (sometimes) with a freer range than the wretched commercial hen. The only way to eat a wild bird is to shoot it yourself, or to find one of the dwindling band of poulterers who handle them.

Some fish, too, are farmed. Between a quarter and a half of all the salmon the world eats are raised by humans. But this has done nothing to reduce the ecological pressure on wild migratory salmon, and the growing indications are that fish farming can and does do fatal damage to its underwater environment. It takes about three kilograms of ground-up fish to produce one kilogram of farmed salmon. Much of this fish meal goes uneaten and joins the steady rain of fish shit on the bed of the bay, loch or fjord where the salmon are penned. The result is pure toxicity, accompanied by algal blooms and epidemic diseases that can spread to wild salmon populations outside. For related reasons, the large-scale, high-intensity shrimp farming that is practised on the mangrove coasts of Thailand, Cambodia, Vietnam and parts of tropical South America has also brought ecological collapse in its train.

But it is largely thanks to the high-tech commercial pursuit of wild fish that the population of the world's oceans is dying, with little prospect of recovery in sight. "In terms of seemliness", wrote James Hamilton-Paterson in his excellent book *The Great Deep: The Sea and Its Thresholds*, "it is no longer possible to propose fish-eating as somehow less objectionable than meat-eating. In terms of ecological damage, the worldwide plundering of marine life may turn out to have been even more disastrous than the felling of rain forest for the benefit of beef ranchers." The world population of fish-eating humans is large enough to bring whole species to the verge of extinction. Modern electronics – gadgets that are the big brothers of the fish finders and sonar units that every inshore amateur or offshore charter skipper has as a matter of course – enable fishing ships to zero in on a pod of albacore 30 kilometres away. They can surprise fish in the previously unreachable quarters of the ocean where they congregate to spawn. The ships can take out huge concentrations of sexually mature fish, on which the future of populations depends. Shallow waters are relentlessly ploughed by beam trawlers, which drag heavy chains across the bottom to harry fish into their nets, thus destroying the bottom-dwelling foods (worms, clams, sea urchins) of future generations and ripping out the weed habitat. In the deep ocean, factory ships up to 100 metres in length, with their own industrial processing and freezing plants on board, draw giant nets that can pull in tens of thousands of fish at a haul. Or the nets are even larger, and left free to float, entangling whatever comes their way. Every night for six months of the year, somewhere between 1,500 and 2,000 ships, in aggregate the world's largest fishing fleet, are at work in the North Pacific. Each of them has laid between 50 and 80 kilometres of drift net, which floats freely in the ocean currents, making in aggregate a shifting, discontinuous and impassable wall of fine nylon monofilament mesh, twelve metres deep and somewhere between 75,000 and 160,000 kilometres in length. Practically nothing can touch this deadly web without being entangled in it: not whales or dolphins, not pelagic fish, not even sea birds. Most of the contents of the drift nets are viewed as waste and dumped overboard, where they die, if they are not dead already. This "by-catch", as it is called, of industrial trawling and drift netting amounts to about a quarter of the total annual catch – 27,000,000 tonnes of waste fish a year. Being creatures of no particular economic interest, these fish become the subjects of what military jargon in the Gulf War called "collateral damage". It is the most conscienceless and indiscriminate way of "harvesting" sea creatures – to use the fatuous euphemism preferred by the fishing industry, which would like you to suppose that the slaughters that ensue were something like the reaping of a renewable crop like wheat – that has ever been devised. But of course, humankind cannot plant new "crops" of bluefin tuna or Pacific salmon; all we can do – in the absence of sufficient internationally agreed and seriously enforceable limits on the catch – is deplete the existing populations so far that their breeding base is damaged or destroyed, which in turn leads to an even more destructive downward spiral of overfishing. Then the pressure moves to other species. Often, little is known about the nature and habits of the newly targeted fish, with unfortunate results. One of the most popular food fishes of recent years has been a deep oceanic dweller called, for its spiny appearance, an orange roughy. Many thousands of tonnes had been hauled from the Pacific before, ten years into the fishery, it was discovered that orange roughies did not attain sexual maturity – and hence could not spawn – until they were 30 years old, and that the specimens of marketable size were probably closer to 100. Overfishing left no backup stock from which the species could regenerate.

In the worst cases, no moratorium on fishing can bring the population back. A complex and insufficiently understood web of ecological factors that had been in place for millions of years before man's impact was felt in the oceans has begun to collapse under stresses it was never designed to absorb. In 1950, according to a 1996 cover report in *Time*, the worldwide catch of oceanic fish was no more than 20 million tonnes a year. By 1989, it was 86 million tonnes, and from that peak it began to drop – the fish populations had reached their limit of exploitation, with too many high-tech fishermen chasing too few fish. That, in essence, is what happened to the once infinite-seeming cod population of the Great Banks; it happened to the fisheries of the North Sea; now it is the Pacific's turn. And the international waters of the Pacific are too big to effectively police. The Japanese, whose government has shown itself to be an entrenched enemy of all serious restrictions on worldwide industrial fishing, knew exactly what to do in the national waters around their coast. There, drift nets have been banned for years.

One single food recipe can imperil a species. The southern redfish, also known as channel bass or drum, *Sciaenops ocellata*, led a fairly balanced collective life, pursued by fishermen both commercial and sporting, but not under excessive pressure, until the early 1980s when a New Orleans cook named Paul Prudhomme created a vogue for something called blackened redfish. The recipe involved taking a fillet of redfish, covering it on both sides with enough hot pepper and herbs to deprive it of any perceptible taste of its own, and then burning it in an iron pan over furious heat until it was encased in a black crust of carbon. This treat (inedible, to my palate, and a standing refutation of Brillat-Savarin's generally sound dictum that the discovery of a new dish brings more happiness to mankind than the discovery of a star) became so widely imitated and consumed throughout the United States that within a few years the redfish was in danger of extinction. Fortunately, restrictions were slapped on the fishery, the vogue passed, and the species seems to have weathered the threat.

Other fish have not fared so well. The case of the bluefin tuna is instructive. 60 years ago, when the Lerners and Farringtons were chasing them for sport, practically the only part of the tuna that a Nova Scotia fisherman could make money on was, strangely enough, the oil in its liver. The mass American palate developed a liking for canned tuna, but that was white-fleshed albacore, not the deep-red bluefin. Even in the late 1960s, on the northeast coast, tuna were not esteemed as a market fish. But then, at the end of the 1970s, the vogue for sushi and sashimi hit American eating habits, and every yuppie from Malibu to SoHo, along with his rail-thin girlfriend, had to learn to eat raw fish, of which the most inviting (because it is red and vaguely beeflike) was a slice of *maguro*, the fillet of flesh from the upper flank of the bluefin, draped over a green dab of wasabi on its lozenge of vinegar-flavoured rice. By the late 1980s, tuna steaks – seared and rare, rather than cooked right through – were bidding fair to replace the proletarian burger on the summer barbecues of Long Island's Hamptons.

Of course, while the round-eyed barbarians were belatedly acquiring a taste for raw tuna, the Japanese had been

fulfilling theirs since the middle Edo period. Millions
upon millions of those tiny red fillets were disappearing
down the collective Japanese throat every day, and to
supply them – since the offshore seas of Japan itself
were effectively fished out – Japanese drift netters and
long-liners were scouring the world's oceans, bringing
back nearly limitless tonnes of *Thunnus thynnus* for home
consumption. They caught them off the Atlantic coast of
the United States and then they caught them in the Gulf
of Mexico, where bluefin go to congregate and spawn. And
from the mid-1980s onward, the docks of Montauk, at the
eastern tip of Long Island, were full of Japanese buyers,
ready to pay unheard-of, unimagined prices, sometimes
100 times the old price, for prime giant bluefin tuna in top
condition. And this was only the tiny visible tip of the
trade, since most Atlantic tuna were and still are caught
by long-liners, not sport fishermen. The big fish would
go into an insulated body bag, and that night it would be
on its way in the hold of a JAL jet to Tokyo, where, fresh
as a daisy, it would appear in the colossal Tsukiji fish
market. Its better cuts of *toro*, the richly fat-marbled belly
meat, auctioned by wholesaler to retailer for $220 or more
a kilogram, would end up in the costlier restaurants at
$75 for two slices the size of your index finger: the
most expensive and sought-after food animal on earth.
A single giant bluefin, 325 kilograms, recently was sold
for $83,500 in Tsukiji. This represents a form of gastro-
nomic fetishism that, in years to come, may seem to
rival the loonier excesses of ancient Roman gastronomy,

such as lark's-tongue pie – though the biomass of bluefin
tuna today certainly exceeds that of Italian larks in
Lucullus's day.

Nevertheless, the bluefin tuna population of the western
Atlantic is collapsing, perhaps to the unsustainable level
at which the breeding stock, if fishing pressure continues,
may never recover. This impending disaster is the result
of greed, denial, political manipulation and sheer supinity
on the part of authorities and organisations whose
supposed task is to protect bluefin stocks. The best account
of it – and of other crises in worldwide fish populations
as well – comes from the marine scientist Dr Carl Safina,
who since 1990 has directed the Living Oceans Program
at the National Audubon Society. His book *Song for the
Blue Ocean* (1997) is the finest thing yet written on ocean
conservation, a remarkable piece of reporting on fish
and those who pursue them on the shores of Europe,
America and Asia. It is written with genuine lyrical power
and underwritten by first-hand experience – Dr Safina is
a fisherman and not merely a dry-seat scientist pushing
numbers through a computer. He relates how an international body set up in the 1960s, representing some 20
Atlantic countries and Japan, which is the largest consumer
of Atlantic tuna, managed to bury and contradict its
own findings on tuna stock. Through its own scientists,
the International Commission for the Conservation of
Atlantic Tunas (ICCAT) learned that the breeding stock
of Atlantic bluefin tuna had declined by almost 90 per
cent since the mid-1970s. They are not the only major

Atlantic species reduced to their lowest level on record. Others include the blue and white marlin, the swordfish, and the yellowfin, bigeye and albacore tunas. One would suppose that this would have caused the gravest anxiety in a conservation and management body such as ICCAT. Apparently not. ICCAT has the power to fix catch quotas, but the only ones it has are for bluefin tuna and swordfish. But, Safina notes with asperity, "those quotas have always been much higher than [its own] scientists recommended – and much higher than the populations could withstand. The commission has in effect presided over the depletion of many of the Atlantic's big fishes. This illustrious résumé suggests that the acronym ICCAT might as well stand for International Conspiracy to Catch All the Tunas."

The destruction of fish populations in the deep oceans is paralleled by the appalling damage done by overfishing along coasts and reefs. The Japanese and others particularly like rich, oily fish such as tuna. In China and much of Southeast Asia, however, the preference is for white-fleshed, flaky fish, particularly the snappers, groupers and wrasses, most of which are reef dwellers. Because the Chinese, in particular, are obsessively finicky about the absolute freshness of their seafood, the fish have to reach the market (and thence, the restaurant) alive, shipped in tanks from the coastal waters of the Philippines, Indonesia, New Guinea and Micronesia. The enormous volume of the live-fish trade in the region relies on the irreversible destruction of their reef habitat. The fish are caught, not with hook and line, not even with nets, but with sodium cyanide, a deadly poison. Divers swim down onto the coral and inject liquid cyanide (supplied by the fish-market middlemen) into its holes and crevices with plastic squirt-bottles. The dazed and disoriented fish come blundering out and are easily taken, though perhaps three-quarters of them (the less commercially valuable species) will be lost on the reef. Transferred to holding pens and thence to tanks, most of the remainder will last long enough to survive the sea voyage (or, for the most valuable fish, the flight) to Hong Kong, Taiwan, Singapore, and their restaurants. Eventually they would die from the cyanide if they were not eaten first. It is something to think about the next time you are in a Chinese restaurant with its aquarium tanks full of fish. Sometimes the fishers – dirt-poor sea peasants, struggling to survive in an inexorably declining fishery – also die from cyanide poisoning. And the reefs, too, perish. Cyanide is supertoxic to coral. Parrotfish eat weed, thus cleaning the coral surface; as their population declines, the coral smothers and dies. Thus the ravenous appetite for reef fish destroys the habitat in which future generations of fish might breed, and the melancholy history of destruction that has been visited on terrestrial species is repeated in the sea. Marine scientists estimate that 90 per cent of the 34,000 square kilometres of coral reef around the Philippine archipelago is dying or already dead from a combination of cyanide fishing, weed overgrowth, industrial pollution and soil runoff from deforested coast. "An active cyanide user", Carl Safina reports, doses fifty coral heads a day, about 225 days a year. In the Philippines alone, some three thousand cyanide users squirt tens of millions of coral heads each year. At this point, just stopping cyanide fishing would be a victory. Never mind catch limits. Never mind quota restrictions. An unrestricted hook-and-line fishery – what we consider uncontrolled, unmanaged fishing in the West – would seem a blessing in the Indo-Pacific, compared to what's now happening here.

Does the sport fisherman, the recreational angler, feel responsible for this situation? Obviously not. Yet both the angler and the industrial fleet share the same oceans and, inevitably, the same fate. There are some kinds of sport fishing that now seem unacceptable, at least to me. In part this is a private matter: I am 60, and as one gets older one views all death with less indifference.

That of a marlin, for instance. Marlin are among the most beautiful creatures in the world, even when they are dead and their colours have gone. But live, in all their power and iridescence, light and water flowing from their bodies, silver and lavender, no words can do them justice: it's like trying to describe an archangel with fins, not wings. When they walk on their tails across the water, or start a plunging run to the horizon, blazing silver amid the white foam, with the line trailing behind in a long catenary, you feel awe at the sight and privilege at being one of the (relatively) few people to see such a thing. But what is this talk of "privilege" when the fish is going to die, after hours of torment, with a razor-barbed #12/0 hook embedded in its gullet or gills? I have never caught a really large billfish, and now if I were offered the chance to do so, I would not take it. The bigger the fish, the less likely it is to survive the ordeal, and the rarer these creatures get, the hollower the desire to catch them becomes. The broadbill swordfish is facing extinction and should be left alone. Marlin taste delicious, and nothing can save them from the Japanese, Taiwanese and Korean long-liners, who inflict an immense carnage upon them, grinding them up to make millions of kilos of fish sausage and fish paste, *surimi*, a year. But one wonders if, from the fish's point of view, there was ever much difference between dying ignominiously on a long line and dying, nobly we are told, on a shorter line connected to Ernest Hemingway, Zane Grey or oneself. The pursuit of big-game records, which inspired the Hemingways and Glassells of another generation, now seems a peculiarly empty form of machismo, however intense the momentary triumph, however mingled its impulses may be with aestheticism. (Nevertheless, I am fairly sure that big-game fishing obsessed Hemingway not because he was a killer but because he was an aesthete, a stylist.) Big-game fishermen, who need to be rich to fish consistently, now spend vast amounts of money chasing what is considered to be the holy grail of such fishing, 2,000-pound black marlin, which have been seen but not caught in the Pacific Ocean off Queensland in Australia. And when one is finally caught, what happens? A statistic

is added to the IGFA records; a tonne of living wildness
is subtracted, forever, from nature. It seems an obscenely
uneven trade-off. And the photographs from the second
third of the twentieth century of big-game champions on
the dock beside their huge dead prey seem, increasingly, to
belong as much to another world as the nineteenth-century
photographs of Indian rajahs and their guest sahibs, or
African white hunters and their clients, posed with the
Bengal tigers and black rhinos they wantonly shot.

I don't want to catch shark, either. In the early 1950s the
idea that sharks were anything but an enemy would have
been regarded by most Australians, and Americans, too,
as insane. And yet, statistically, they posed far less threat
to human life than did crossing a suburban street. The idea
that shark fishermen made the water safer for swimmers
was the merest flummery, without a jot of evidence to back
it up. You might as well defend elephant or lion killing in
Africa on the grounds that the death of these magnificent
quadrupeds makes it safer for people to wander as they
please on the veldt. So it might – very marginally. But what
of it? After Steven Spielberg's *Jaws*, that witless knockoff
of *Moby Dick*, became a smash hit, Americans went into
prolonged shark shock. They were happy that after years
of listening to conservationists' lectures on the sanctity of
Nature, Hollywood had given them something natural to
hate – *Carcharodon carcharias*, the great white, six metres
of insatiable appetite and rampant id, the mother of all
otherness. Armies of middle-aged dentists from New
Jersey, bursting with testosterone, sallied forth to Montauk

to hire boats and prove what tough guys they were by hauling in a shark, any shark, though preferably a great white. Charter captains, notably Frank Mundus, supposedly the Ahab figure on whom the obsessed shark-chaser of *Jaws* was modelled, made their retirement money off this reverse feeding frenzy. No catch-and-release here: you can't release a gut-hooked shark, you have to kill it. And then, for want of anything better to do with its carcass, string it up and have your photo taken with it before it goes in the fish-meal grinder. As a sporting spectacle, this had all the allure of watching dogs being bludgeoned to death in a pool.

Nor was the practice rendered any more edifying by the thought of the wholesale slaughter of sharks on the other side of the world – by Southeast Asian and Japanese long-liners, for instance, who haul in countless thousands of sharks every week, hack off their fins to be dried for Chinese soup, and dump the still-living, helpless bodies back in the ocean. Big sharks have few defenders, but now they need all they can get, though they don't know it. At least the Australian Government has declared the great white a protected species, along with the saltwater crocodile, the largest and most dangerous reptile on earth, which until 1971 was being shot to extinction. That is as it should be, for we have no moral right to preserve only cuddly tourist attractions like the koala. Wildness, otherness and dread, embodied in living creatures, also have their claims. It is beneficial, if you find yourself casting a fly for barramundi from an aluminium dinghy in the waters of a north Australian coastal billabong, to see a saltie longer than the boat swim by. It puts you in your place. For that, it is worth losing the occasional careless tourist.

Take the fear and trembling out of Nature and you're left with Disney World. The "watery part of the world", as Herman Melville called it, is a zone of fear and trembling, as well as a place of endless curiosity, fascination and delight. The waters teach us that we are not the lords of the universe, with all other living creatures our vassals and serfs. The Genesis account of creation – God setting man in dominion over the Earth and all its creatures – has become one of the most destructive myths ever to encumber the human mind. We are part of a chain of being, or rather a vastly intricate net, whose integrity we violate to our own peril as individuals and as a species. It is a lesson driven home repeatedly by conservationists on land, but although it applies just as forcibly to the sea its application there is less understood. We need to understand it. Angling, at its best, is a means to that understanding.

There is no defensible ethic or aesthetic of angling that doesn't centre on moderation. Just as a properly trained hunter should never point his gun, let alone fire a shot, at a living animal that he doesn't intend to eat, so an angler should never kill a fish that will not reach the table in a state of perfect freshness. The others can be released. Which means that you should always stop – stop killing, not necessarily fishing – when you have enough on the beach or in the live well to feed you and yours for the next day or two. This does not diminish the pleasure of the

sport. Rather, it enhances it. Who really needs all that
dead seafood? Just as there is one moment in the life of
a peach when it is perfectly ripe, so the special pleasure
of eating fish arises when you have caught the creature
yourself and it is just out of the water. Offering your friends
a poached striped bass that you caught yesterday evening
is qualitatively different from feeding them one you
bought in a shop. No flatfish ever tasted as good to me as
the flounder I would fillet on board a friend's ancient
rust bucket on Long Island's Peconic Bays, then wrap
in aluminium foil with a pinch of salt and pepper, and
cook on the engine manifold. Of all the sashimi I have
eaten over the years, the best was on Alan Shields' boat
off Montauk. Having brought wasabi, soy sauce, and my
second-best *deba-bocho* (sushi knife) along, I would take
a thin slice or two off the flank of a just-caught yellowfin
tuna and, after admiring the rainbow glimmer of transected
fibres in the flesh (like a diffraction grating), gobble it
down for breakfast. I may sound like a fanatic, but I disap-
prove of home-freezing surplus fish. The end product can't
be distinguished from what you can buy in a market, so
why bother?

A sense of moderation invites you to scale down your
tackle, to accept the gratification of medium success with
more demanding techniques in place of a big bag: lighter
lines, thinner rods, saltwater flies instead of live baits or
spun lures. Nobody really respects a meat fisherman, except
other meat fishermen. Official record sizes don't matter
anymore – not, at least, to the fishers I know. It is better to

release a fish than to keep it, even when minimum-size rules permit you to keep it. A rhyme from my childhood, read in some fishing anthology, sticks in my head:

> Enjoy the stream, thou harmless Fish!
> And when the angler, for his dish,
> Through Gluttony's vile sin,
> Attempts (the wretch) to pull thee out,
> God give thee strength, thou gentle Trout,
> To pull the Rascal in.

I don't know that I'd quite endorse that – I am too gluttonous to do so without hypocrisy – but one gets the point. The joy of fishing is in the catching, not the killing; and, much of the time, in the not-catching as well, the absorption in Nature. Anglers see only a tiny corner of the vast life of the world's waters. But what they do see, they are apt to see thoroughly. Isaak Walton and his successors were right about that. Sometimes the empty cooler contains the finest sashimi.

INDEX